Praise for Ilya Kutik's *Hieroglyphs of Another World*:

"From Paul Valery to Yvor Winters, poets have often made singularly eccentric contributions to prose. Russian poet Ilya Kutik throws his hat into the contemporary ring with the intriguing collection *Hieroglyphs of Another World: On Poetry, Swedenborg, and Other Matters*. . . . Though unpredictable, Kutik's style never becomes forbiddingly esoteric, and his critical ideas veer more toward the delightful . . . than the ponderous."
—*Publishers Weekly*

"Kutik is a formidable talent. Like Joseph Brodsky's, his English is strikingly eccentric and all the more effective for that very reason. The same can be said for his style, which layers metaphor on metaphor drawn from a formidably eclectic reservoir of cultures, with Russian as the core layer."
—*Choice*

"[. . .]Kutik proclaims that he is a fatalist, because just as rhyme and rhythm are correspondences at play, so are the events of life, the poet's favorite playthings. . . . Paradox subverts the apparent meaning of an occurrence . . . but it teaches us to appreciate the Whole, and that is . . . what the contemporary student of literature needs."
—*Slavic and East European Journal*

Writing as Exorcism

Northwestern University Press
Studies in Russian Literature and Theory

Series Editors
   Robert Belknap
   Caryl Emerson
   Gary Saul Morson
   William Mills Todd III
   Andrew Wachtel

Writing as Exorcism

THE PERSONAL CODES OF PUSHKIN,
LERMONTOV, AND GOGOL

Ilya Kutik

NORTHWESTERN UNIVERSITY PRESS / EVANSTON, ILLINOIS

Northwestern University Press
Evanston, Illinois 60208-4210

Copyright © 2005 by Northwestern University Press.
Published 2005. All rights reserved.

Printed in the United States of America

10 9 8 7 6 5 4 3 2 1

ISBN 0-8101-2051-8

Library of Congress Cataloging-in-Publication data are available
from the Library of Congress.

The paper used in this publication meets the minimum requirements of the American National Standard for Information Sciences—Permanence of Paper for Printed Library Materials, ANSI Z39.48-1992.

Contents

Introduction by Gary Saul Morson		vii
Chapter One	Exorcism and "the Extra" in the Text	3
Chapter Two	Two Superstitious Men	14
Chapter Three	Gogol's Nausea and Nossea	53
Chapter Four	Rome before Rome	84
Conclusion: Musings on Modifications of Exorcism		118
Notes		131
Works Cited		141
Index		145

Gary Saul Morson

Introduction: Reading the Extra

Sometimes it takes a poet to read a poet.

In this inspired, idiosyncratic study, Ilya Kutik offers exemplary interpretations of three Russian writers, of the lessons of fatalism, and of the complexities of reading. Interestingly enough, though Kutik focuses on literary texts, examines them almost atomistically, and discovers important but missed intertextual references, he professes to contribute nothing to the understanding of literature. More accurately, such contributions—and there are many—emerge as mere by-products of what really interests him: the "extra." Once one grasps what he means by this term, one may well imagine other possible extras. In order to see where Kutik's ideas might lead, it would be helpful to situate them in critical history.

When twentieth-century criticism is assessed, historians may decide that its greatest contribution was theories of readers and reading. As far back as the 1910s, the Russian Formalists defined literature (or "literariness") as verbal work that "bestranges": if a work makes you see the world as if for the first time—things as they are immediately felt, not as they are habitualized and "known"—then it is art for you. But once a given kind of bestrangement itself becomes routine, then, though called art by habit, it ceases to function as such. Those for whom the technique is still new experience such works as art, while older hands hold literary historical documents. The readership doubles.

Russian thinkers of the 1910s and 1920s, as well as European and American ones decades later, focused on the reader's response (or was it the readers' response?) as somehow essential to literature. Literature ceased to be a thing and became a transaction. It was only one step from here to performance art or, let us say, to J. S. G. Boggs's use of drawings of money, along with receipts and merchandise purchased for it by astute merchants, as artworks in themselves.[1] But how are we to understand the reader's activity? What exactly does the reader do, and what is his or her role in a literary transaction? How much like buying and selling are writing and reading? Or

Introduction

is interpretation simply a form of decoding, with the reader simply extracting the message placed there by the author like a telegraph office rendering Morse code back into words?

The decoding hypothesis, in endless variations, has produced a vast array of sophisticated work, from Yuri Tynyanov and Roman Jakobson to Wolfgang Iser and numerous French or American structuralists. Part of this model's appeal lies in separating sheep from goats. Just as Morse code can be deciphered correctly or incorrectly, and with more or less of the message recovered, so literary interpretation could be more or less successful depending on the skill of experts—ourselves, of course—propounding the theory. We, and we alone, can assume the role of perfect decoder: the ideal reader, *c'est moi.*

For a kabbalist, a conspiracy detector, or a scholar, such a model has an understandable appeal. But what if the author has enjoyed a vast *popular* audience, as Dickens and Trollope did? Are we to say that the very audience for whom they wrote were uncomprehending, whereas the critic who unearths obscure meanings has appreciated them? There is something evidently implausible about this approach, however much recourse is made to the unconscious, the text, or language as such.

The decoding model, therefore, also doubles the readership into the knowing and unknowing and thus serves as a ticket to pedagogic employment. But if the ideal reader decodes ideally, why do ideal readers so often disagree? How can it be that a sophisticated method for resolving interpretive disputes multiplies rather than reduces them? In *War and Peace,* Pierre accepts Freemasonry because it provides the key to the mysteries, resolves all disputes, and so promises universal brotherhood. It turns out, however, that Freemasons themselves interpret their creed variously. When Pierre's speech to the lodge provokes a row, he finds himself deeply depressed not by those who disagree with him but by those who agree:

> At this meeting Pierre for the first time was struck by the endless variety of men's minds, which prevents a truth from ever appearing the same to any two persons. Even those members who seemed to be on his side understood him in their own way, with stipulations and modifications he could not agree to, since what he chiefly desired was to convey his thought to others exactly as he himself understood it.[2]

But exact coincidence of understanding is impossible, because understanding is a form of appropriation to one's self, with all the particular experiences that have formed it, and no two selves are identical. For Pierre, this realization spells doom for his dream of utopia, and for the literary theorist it shatters the dream of objectivity. Arise subjectivism: Norman Holland and others stressed the unrepeatable parts of the reading experience. But such an approach failed to do justice to the sense that some readings really are better than others, which suggests that literature is not wholly subjective. And if it were, who would need professors of literature?

So the "interpretive community" was discovered. In America, we associate this idea with Stanley Fish; in Russia, it was pioneered in the late 1920s by Boris Eichenbaum, who stressed how different O. Henry's stories are to Russian readers. Eichenbaum's observations were extended by Prague theorists of the 1930s before Fish announced them. But what exactly is a readership?

Familiar answers were at hand. Perhaps all readerships are in principle equal: each set of interpretive criteria appears convincing to those who hold it. Or perhaps certain groups of readers have special insight by virtue of their "race, gender, class" or professional training: along with theory, oppression (or descent) confers abstruse interpretive capabilities. Or perhaps both: all readings are equal, but some are more equal than others. They are equal in principle, but those with "power" may make them true; and since there are no criteria other than power, the only question is who wields the sword or pays the professor. The cynicism of this approach figures as sophistication. Like the sensitive Jewish commissar in Isaac Babel's *Red Cavalry* stories, its proponents justify vicariously the mentality of Cossacks. Readerships are again divided, this time into those foolish enough to believe in better methods and those wise enough to advance their careers.

Perhaps the most interesting version of reader reception theory belongs to Mikhail Bakhtin, who knew all about power. To this anti-Marxist Soviet citizen of bourgeois background, "the death of the author" was no mere metaphor. Russia has this unfortunate habit of doing what Western intellectuals protected by bourgeois institutions advocate. In the high Stalin years and after, Bakhtin developed a theory of literary interpretation that gives individual readers and specific readerships an active role and yet allows for interpretations to be better or worse responses to a literary work.

Bakhtin described three kinds of reading. First, scholars typically "enclose" a writer "in his epoch": they discover the meanings that the author knew or might have known consciously or unconsciously. Second, readers, especially those impressed with the wisdom of their time, practice "modernization and distortion" by imposing upon the work gratifying interpretations it cannot sustain. Thus far we are on familiar territory. But there is a third kind of reading, which depends on Bakhtin's idea of dialogue.

Here what is doubled is the author's intention. Each great work contains both *meanings* that the author could have known and *potentials* of which he or she is aware. These potentials are one side of a dialogue. They are really in the work, but they require a dialogic partner—from another

Introduction

culture or age—to activate them. Genuine dialogue generates the new. Since other cultures and ages are infinitely various, so are the potential meanings of the work. But it is a (common) fallacy to assume that if a work's potential meanings are infinite, they include *every* imaginable meaning. Consider: a line contains an infinite number of points, but not every point. And so a work's meanings may be infinite but still exclude some interpretations. In Bakhtin's model, unless readers engage in dialogue with the potentials that are actually in the work, they engage simply in modernization and distortion, narcissistically reproducing what they already know and so learning nothing new.

Writers thus *intend* both specific meanings and the potential for more meanings: they sense this potential as a kind of richness. They can recognize it because, as readers, they have responded to it in other works. Tradition's importance lies in its wealth of elements, themes and forms rich in potential, that have accumulated over "great time." Decayed literature makes the richest soil. Although Bakhtin does not explicitly say so, the presence of such potentials may be a criterion of greatness. A work without them, a work that simply says what the author wished to say, cannot grow and will die with its age, for that which exists only in the present is bound to die with the present.

All these models deal with the meanings of a literary work, but no work is *only* literary. I am referring not to its political or social impact, because those depend on first interpreting the work as literature, however inadequately. Rather, I have in mind the central thesis of Kutik's book: that a writer may create a masterpiece that functions both as literature and as something "extra," to use Kutik's term. Remarkably, Kutik disclaims any intention to reveal the meaning of literary works. Whatever interpretation you have of *The Queen of Spades, Dead Souls,* or *A Hero of Our Time* remains untouched by his analysis. The point is worth stressing because earlier—and I suspect later—readers of this study complain that it contradicts "other" interpretations. But it does not even engage them.

Let me clarify what Kutik does and does not mean to say. Some (by no means all) works address themselves as literature to one kind of reader and as a specific type of nonliterature to another, much as, let us say, a given mask, weapon, or work of architecture may serve artistic and nonartistic functions. Except that those analogues do not really hit the mark: a building's artistic effect may be part of its appeal as a habitation, and a weapon may dazzle before it strikes. In those cases, the artistic and nonartistic functions of the artifact overlap and may even complement each other. Kutik is speaking of cases where the two functions are entirely distinct, perhaps even at odds.

In this respect, Kutik's "extras" resemble the hidden meanings of

Introduction

"Aesopian literature," a term Russians (since Saltykov-Shchedrin) have used to describe writing designed to appear orthodox to the censor but betray itself to a readership in the know. This venerable tradition had its dangers. Since not all censors or police officials were idiots, they might detect the hidden meanings; and whether idiots or not, they might, and often did, "discover" subversive meanings in texts that were in fact innocent of them. Or were they? Current literary theory could make a prosecutorial case. No matter what the author thought he meant, perhaps his unconscious spoke otherwise or his language deconstructed itself? And if meaning belongs to communities of readers, surely the *nomenklatura* and its agents constituted a community; and they did, after all, have power. The fact is that when Aesopian interpretation is common, it can always be ascribed; and, whatever meanings you suspect, you will find interpretive methods to demonstrate them. Such a dynamic is, I take it, the point Dostoevsky makes in the title of one *Writer's Diary* article: "The Thirst for Rumors and for 'What is Concealed.' The Phrase 'What Is Concealed' May Have a Future, and Measures Should Be Taken in Advance" (July–August 1877, chapter 1, article 2).

Yet even this example of nonoverlapping readerships does not match the ones Kutik describes. To begin with, the hidden readership of Aesopian works may still be reading the work as literature and simply interpreting it in a nonstraightforward way. Moreover, such groups of readers are precisely that, *groups* of readers, whereas Kutik has in mind a single reader, a community of one: Aesopian language designed only for Aesop.

The sole reader who is meant to understand is the author, for whom the work constitutes both a literary effort for a general readership and a sort of private prayer or exorcism that he alone (or he and Fate) is to detect. Somehow the intensely superstitious Pushkin, whose witty works mocked the superstitions of his characters, made those very works into amulets for himself. Believing in fate, he hoped to turn *The Queen of Spades* into a way of avoiding his destiny, as revealed by a fortune-teller. And yet, as a literary work, no such meaning appears. If anything, the very opposite is the case: those who believe in hidden keys come to destruction.

For such a spell as Pushkin's to work, readers must not be aware of it. As Kutik sums up, the authors intend themselves to be "fully *sighted*, but they want us to remain *blind*. My task here is to try to reveal their secrets."

So is this another form of Freudianism? Not at all: Kutik has in mind precisely those meanings the author deliberates. Far from being unconscious, they require intense labor to plant while still making the work successful, on quite other grounds, as literature.

Kutik's readings, then, add nothing to our understanding of literary works. Instead, they contribute to our understanding of their authors. Kutik's method is a special, weird form of biographism, which avoids the usual pitfalls of that approach. Authors of biographical studies—Freud and his disciples come to mind—too often reduce the work to the life, especially its less than appealing moments. If we derive a smug sense of superiority to a genius we understand better than he knew himself, we do so by a kind of reverse Midas touch: "anal retentiveness" turns the gold to shit. The best biographers, such as Joseph Frank in his multivolume life of Dostoevsky, do the reverse: use the life to make the works even richer. I remain convinced that biography, if appropriately practiced, and where evidence is available, can do that, and can more or less bridge the gap between a private drama and a public masterpiece. To do so, it would help to understand the creative process, that is, just how the author grew out of his or her experience. We too frequently forget that the act of writing is itself a part of the life and, for a great writer, the most important part.

Kutik's study reveals the genuine oddity of Pushkin, Lermontov, and Gogol. God knows whether they were larger than life, but they were certainly larger than literature. And the nature of their vital drama feels Russian to the extreme. Take Pushkin, for instance, who, in Kutik's account, believed he was fated to die at age thirty-seven—unless he could survive death that crucial year at the hands of a blond man on account of his wife. Thus *The Queen of Spades* features a strange numerology with a three and a seven, its author believing that his story had exorcised his fate. To find out, he courted death as a test; and so, at age thirty-seven, he died at the hands of a blond man on account of his wife.

Russian cultural history often seems like a persistent dialogue with fatalism. Teleological historical materialism is only the most obvious example. That version of fatalism paralyzed numerous liberal intellectuals who knew better. How, they asked themselves, could they resist History, the inevitable future? Russia resembles Pushkin's Hermann, whose belief that he can outwit chance and guess three cards in advance clearly symbolizes the ability to control the uncontrollable future. Like Raskolnikov and the narrator of Dostoevsky's *The Gambler,* and like the real-life gamblers with history in the twentieth century, Pushkin's hero believes he can leap from the kingdom of necessity to the kingdom of freedom; but unlike the revolutionaries, the madness to which he succumbs affects only himself, not untold millions.

Fatalism takes countless forms, and none of us is quite immune to it. Its language and trappings change, but its appeal remains. How many people succumb to a fate made by their belief in it? Was our self formed by age five and are we governed not by our will but by our unconscious, as some Freudians tell us? The iron laws of history shackle, above all, their adherents. But the chains they forge enslave others. That is the odd thing about social laws: chemicals do not alter their behavior to accord with or refute our theories about them, but people do. In *Anna Karenina,* the eponymous

Introduction

heroine believes in the fatalism of Romantic love, prophetic dreams, and secret omens. Tolstoy is careful to reveal that Anna jumps under the train not because an omen is fulfilled but because she *thinks* of the omen and realizes "what she had to do." Not her fate but her fatalism kills her.

Yet the majority of this book's readers have missed the point and seen Anna as implacably doomed by a Romantic destiny. Perhaps they have told themselves something similar, and used inevitability as a consolation or excuse. Where fatalism rules, there is no room for regret, no good and evil. If open time does not exist, then all is permitted. Perhaps Russian history, and the amazing fatalistic lives Kutik reveals, could forestall our succumbing to fatalism, no matter how artfully or "scientifically" reclad; but I doubt it. Those whom the gods would destroy they first endow with destiny.

Writing as Exorcism

Chapter One

Exorcism and "the Extra" in the Text

APPROACH TO THE TERM: WHAT IS EXORCISM?

In 1973, the movie *The Exorcist,* directed by William Friedkin, became part of the American horror film classic tradition. In the film, a priest, played by Ingmar Bergman's famous actor Max von Sydow, fights the Devil (who has moved into a young girl's body) with the magic of special incantations, that is, with the power of *words*. The Devil fights back, forcing the girl to fly over the bed. She responds to the spells with a thunderous voice from lips that bubble with a great deal of artificial green saliva and lifts the priest off the floor like a feather. Naturally, the exorcisms finally succeed in casting out the Devil.

There is exorcism and then there is exorcism. The type of exorcism that I will discuss in this book has nothing to do with special effects and satanic possession of human bodies. However, it does have to do with the power of words, which is what literature shares with classic exorcism. To put it a bit differently, this book is about *personal* exorcisms, the ones writers perform while fighting on paper with their inner demons, fears, and even fate and death. The writer embarks upon this fight in order either to eradicate these troubles or, on the contrary, to attract desired events. This process is designedly concealed from the audience and is apparent only to the one who performs it, that is, the author. Moreover, I use "exorcism" here as a term not only for the process but also for the *result* of writing. This result is a text in which an author's exorcising strategy is reflected. The question I am interested in asking here is, why does a particular type of writer write? What does he or she do it for?

Of course, the author's desire for self-expression would be an immediate answer to the question about his reasons for writing. But what does this notorious self-expression specifically mean? What forms does it take inside the text? Is it the text itself? To be sure, many authors write because they simply cannot avoid the process, cannot and do not want to resist the impulse to start writing. Obviously, for such writers the process is in itself a necessity, sometimes a tormenting one. We know that all writers write for others to some extent. But those writers who perform exorcisms, as we will see, also write for themselves. They add something "extra" to their texts, something not meant to be perceived but nevertheless perceivable if one knows how to look. My book is about that "extra" in the text. I call it the *psychological dominant,* with/against which some authors deal/struggle in a given literary work. A given author's psychological dominant forms the basis of his or her personal code.

This specific type of authorial concern with or struggle against the psychological dominant is present only in a certain group of writers and their texts. In this book I investigate just a few works, all well known, by Alexander Pushkin, Mikhail Lermontov, and Nikolai Gogol. Although all three authors belong to the Romantic period of Russian literature, that is, to the first half of the nineteenth century, I do not claim that Romanticism as a literary or philosophical movement explains why they use their texts to perform a personal exorcism. To my mind, the ideology or mindset of specific literary periods or schools has almost nothing to do with it. To be sure, certain periods, Romanticism among them, focus the writer's interest in and concern for the psychological dominant, because the very tendencies of a given era may accentuate the uniqueness of the creative personality and provoke a heightened attention to all that is fantastic and transcendental. However, there were undoubtedly many Romantic authors who did not use literature for personal exorcism, just as there are authors in other periods who did. There must be a different explanation having little to do with the overall literary and cultural time period for why only some writers perform personal exorcisms. How can we characterize these writers?

The works under discussion in this book are for the most part prose fiction. Nevertheless, two of the authors, Pushkin and Lermontov, although eminent prose writers, started their careers as poets and remain the most celebrated poets of nineteenth-century Russia. Gogol, who is now known solely as a prose writer, also started his literary career as a poet, although his early verse works were disastrous failures. Moreover, Gogol's complex of failure as a poet was fully mirrored in his approach to prose. Thus, for example, Gogol called his masterpiece, the novel *Dead Souls,* a *poema,* that is, an epic poem. The Russian writer Viktor Sosnora has aptly noted about Gogol: "He is very mysterious, without age; at the age of twenty-two he was already writing like Homer."[1] In many respects, Gogol was the first Russian "poet in prose."

Thus, all three writers who are the subjects of this book fit into the group of authors who approach prose through the lens of poetry. This means that they trust the transcendent power of words no less than they do, for example, their own ability to originate plot, characters, and scenes. In their

Exorcism and "the Extra" in the Text

turn, as we will have abundant opportunity to see, in the works of these authors both plot and characters often grow out of either wordplay or some purely linguistic logic. Moreover, the exploitation of the multiplicity of the poetic word gives the writers in question the opportunity to create in their texts various additional meanings that can be traced, or revealed, only if we recreate the ways in which they were thinking while writing, that is, their associational, often extremely paradoxical and idiosyncratic moves.

The readings that follow are unabashedly idiosyncratic themselves. As a practicing poet, I myself have experienced some of the same desires and used my texts in the ways I claim that Pushkin, Lermontov, and Gogol used theirs, and I use my poetic intuition to recreate what I believe to have been the mindsets of these authors as they wrote. Thus, in performing the readings presented here, I try to percolate through the text to the author's mentality and, more broadly, into his life concerns. I do believe that my intuitive discoveries lead to provocative readings of the literary works treated. But they do so from the inside out, as it were, beginning from the premise that it is possible to recover, at least in part, the exorcism that an author performs for himself and, perhaps, for God or some metaphysical power, which it is hoped will take into account the author's fears or wishes. Significantly, this type of creative process is fully *conscious:* the author knows precisely that *which* he exorcises; the author does not suppress or repress his secret fears or wishes, but, on the contrary, splashes them out on paper and thus struggles with them.

This approach may seem to some readers overly impressionistic. To this I can only reply that I do use standard literary critical approaches, particularly intertextual and biographical ones, and nothing I propose here contradicts the textual evidence available. This is inevitable, since the only material I have for the recovery of a given author's psychological dominant is his own texts and texts by those who interacted with him. Thus, I would say that what some may see as my flights of fancy are merely a recreation of the creative fantasies of three authors of genius.

To give an initial example of what I have in mind, let us turn to Nikolai Gogol.

EXAMPLE 1: EXORCISING A NAME

For his poetic debut of 1829, the long narrative poem "Ganz Küchelgarten," Gogol (full name Nikolai Vasilievich Gogol-Ianovskii) chose the pseudonym V. Alov, whose probable meaning I discuss in the beginning of chapter 3. In 1831, Gogol published three more prose pieces, again under various pseudonyms. They are the fragment "Teacher" (From the Ukrainian novella "A

Frightful Boar") under the name P. Glechyk (in Ukrainian, *glechyk* means "pitcher"); the essay "A Few Thoughts about How to Teach Children Geography," signed G. Ianov; and finally "Chapters from the Novel *Hetman*" under the strangest nom de plume: 0000.

Speaking about the last of these, Gogol's early biographer P. Kulish explains its oddity by the presence of four *o*s in the writer's first and double-last names: NikOlai GOgOl-IanOvsky.[2] As a visual phenomenon, this explanation looks like an anticipation of a line from E. E. Cummings and at first glance convincingly traces the associational moves that urged Gogol to create this pseudonym. However, it should be noted that when sending the chapters from *Hetman* to his mother Gogol himself emphasized in the enclosed letter that his prose "is signed by four zeroes,"[3] not four *o*s. Why is this important?

In Gogol's case, the difference, I think, is crucial. By using precisely zeroes instead of an articulate human name, Gogol hints at the fact that the writer is a zero himself, that is, that he is a noman. This kind of anonymity leads us to that episode in the *Odyssey* of Homer (Gogol's favorite author) in which Odysseus answers Polyphemus's request for his name by saying that he is Noman. When the other Cyclopses, in their turn, ask Polyphemus who blinded him, he says that noman did. Probably, by signing his prose 0000, Gogol simply wanted to point out that he, the true literary conqueror, has already come to existence but that he prefers to remain nameless, like Odysseus. Still, two questions remain to be asked here: why are there four zeroes? And why did Gogol wish to remain an undesignated writer?

A conceivable explanation for the former might be connected to the fact that Gogol made exactly four anonymous debuts. Only his fifth prose work, a Romantic fantasia on the antique topic entitled "Woman," came out under his real name. This also happened in 1831, and almost simultaneously with the fourth one, which was signed 0000. However, the latter had already been approved by the censorship in 1830, and thus it *is* Gogol's fourth published work.[4] Four times running Gogol pretended that he was a ghostwriter; only then did he decide to announce that he was indeed Gogol. Why such a restraint?

The reason, I believe, is a particular mental twist, or psychological dominant, in Gogol: he did not turn to pseudonyms simply because of the fear of being underestimated by his real name, or the shyness of a debutante (although both of these factors may also have been present). In so doing, Gogol behaves as one who understands the Old Testament personally and literally: if God cannot be called by his real name, why should I? This way of reading the Bible—that is, as a literal and personal document—was characteristic of Gogol and is manifest in his last published work, *Selected Passages from Correspondence with Friends*. It also suggests that Gogol treated his own self as a divine one—not a very unusual attitude for a writer, who *is* after all a creator. However, Gogol goes much further than normal. He is remarkably open and conscious about his self-deification, although *only* to himself and not to his audience (at least until the time of *Selected Passages* in which he is openly the Teacher—but even then, not God!).

In 1830 and 1831, the period when he used pseudonyms and finally his real name, Gogol wrote an essay titled "Boris Godunov." Despite the fact that its topic was fashionable thanks to Pushkin's recently published drama, the essay, not published until 1881, remained unknown during Gogol's lifetime. Why? Because in it Gogol is completely frank and blasphemous: he is a God, or at least he is God's equal. "If the sky, the sun-rays, the ocean, the fires eating the intestines of our earth, the endless air embracing worlds, the angels, the inflamed planets were all transformed into words and letters—even then I would not be able to express a tenth part of those amazing things taking place in the bosom of the *invisible me.* And what are they in the comparison with the human soul? with God's embodiment? [emphasis Gogol's]"⁵

Thus, according to Gogol, he *is* "invisible," that is, a zero, but the invisible *everything,* that is, a god.

A complementary explanation of Gogol's fear of using his name might be connected to the accident of that very name as such. With his oversensitive ear, it is highly unlikely that the similarity between his own name and that of Gog, the Old Testament precursor to the Antichrist, could have possibly escaped Gogol. According to the book of Ezekiel (chapters 38–39), Gog will arise as Jehovah's rival at the end of the world, predicting the appearance of the Antichrist. As a very pious person, Gogol was most probably afraid of this coincidence. Understanding himself as God's equal, he must have been scared by this coincidence even more.

And here Gogol's exorcism starts. Because he believes in the divine concept of himself yet is fully aware of the theological implications of such an idea, he continually tries to exorcise his pride. He resembles a monk who whips himself because he has sinned or because his thoughts were sinful, although Gogol's self-flagellation takes place only on paper (not for nothing; in *The Inspector General* we meet a character, though female, who has whipped herself). And even when using his true name instead of various pseudonyms, Gogol nevertheless tries to escape from it, that is, to depersonify it, to melt into something impersonal. Thus, in the finale of "Taras Bulba" we meet the author in a very strange capacity: he is not a person but rather a "golden-eyed duck" (*gogol* in Russian means "this bird"). Moreover, he gives this duck a special character: ". . . and the *proud* golden-eye duck soars swiftly above it [the Dniester river] [emphasis added]." In so doing, Gogol exorcises his name (he is again depersonified, a "zero"), but he cannot resist the sinful characterization of himself as a "proud" man.

Gogol's attraction toward a zero situation is truly amazing. In *Dead Souls,* landlords trade dead serfs, that is, zeroes, and their purchaser Chichikov is a zero, too. About him, Gogol writes: "The gentleman lolling back in the chaise was neither dashingly handsome nor yet unbearably ugly, neither too stout nor yet too thin; it could not be claimed that he was old, but he was no stripling either. His arrival in the town created no stir and was not marked by anything out of the ordinary."[6] In other words, Chichikov is "neither-nor," that is, a noman. Moreover, the next passage of the "poem" touches on a wheel of Chichikov's chaise, that is, also a zero. A zero arrives in the town riding a zero. Because the work is both comical and prophetic (at least, Gogol planned it this way), in Chichikov he once again exorcises his own pride, this time with laughter. He creates the worst possible zero in order to prove to himself that his is not the only way to be a noman.

I have already said that one of Gogol's psychological dominants was his fear of his own name. We know that Gogol used pseudonyms constantly, and his last one was the most puzzling: 0000. If we use an intertextual approach it will be discovered that, according to his biographer Kulish, 0000 meant four *os*, while according to the author's own letter they mean four zeroes. Biographically this is reasonable because this was the fourth of Gogol's pseudonyms. However, if we continue with both biographical and intertextual analyses, we find out that Homer was Gogol's favorite author (a biographical fact) and that this fact leads to Odysseus's pseudonym: Noman (intertextuality). Thus, zero is also a noman.

Still, why was Gogol afraid of his real name? From his unpublished essay, we find out that he treated himself as a divine creature (intertextuality). This leads us to the Bible, in which God could not be called by his own name (intertextuality). It also leads us to a book in the Bible in which a kind of Antichrist is called Gog, that is, almost by Gogol's name (intertextuality). Gogol's fear becomes even clearer: he thinks of himself as practically God's equal (we know from the essay), but as a pious man (a biographical fact) he is afraid of himself as an Antichrist. This is his personal code. He was, first, *conscious* about his self-deification (he wrote about it in the essay); second, he tried to *conceal* this sinful self-attitude (he did not publish the essay). Because it is sinful and because he is the namesake of the Antichrist, Gogol starts his exorcism on paper—in order to get rid of his fear and pride. However, he is already known by his real name (a biographical fact). That is why, in one of his works of epic character, he shows himself in a homonym, *gogol*-as-duck (intertextuality), and thus "humiliates" the name. Nevertheless, he calls this duck a "proud" one—the ambiguity of Gogol's approach to himself. He continues to exorcise this pride—of a noman = God's equal. He creates zero-situations and zero-characters, which are the worst possible nomen, and thus a "normal" self-humiliation.

Exorcism and "the Extra" in the Text

As we have seen, a psychological dominant—via biographical fact—is the first step to the discovery of an author's personal code. The latter is possible to determine if we combine biographical facts and intertextuality. After this code is found, we try to establish an author's associational links—step three—which will lead us to his exorcism, that is, the *reason* for, the *process* of, and the *result* of it. Neither Gogol's life alone (the fact of his prolific use of pseudonyms) nor the texts themselves are sufficient to provide an explanation of what Gogol writes or why he behaves the way he does. If we combine all three steps we will be able to answer to the question I asked in the very beginning: why does the author write what he writes? In Gogol's case as well as in those of similar authors, the answer to my question would be to exorcise their psychological dominants on paper, that is, their secret fears, wishes, and so forth.

EXAMPLE 2: DELIVERANCE FROM NOSTALGIA

The reader will find other examples of writing as exorcism in the course of this book. For me, however, it is important to point out that authorial exorcism can be discovered not just in writing, but in other arts as well. As an example, let us turn to film.

In 1983, Andrei Tarkovsky, probably one of the greatest directors of our time, shot *Nostalgia,* a very mysterious film about a Russian man abroad. In 1984, Tarkovsky, then a citizen of the USSR, asked for asylum in Italy, where he had stayed since shooting *Nostalgia.* In 1986, after shooting one more film in Sweden, he died in France at age fifty-four. Those are some biographical facts, and now we consider the film.

Its protagonist, Gorchakov, is a poet. He comes to Italy in order to collect material for his opera libretto. Driven by nostalgia, Gorchakov can no longer face the various beauties of the country; he is totally swallowed by the feeling, lost in it. At some point, he meets Domenico, whom everybody takes for a holy fool. He is a former mathematician, but now is evidently crazy. They become friends. Domenico believes that the world will be destroyed soon because it is insane, and that, because people in this world are separated, they must all be rescued together. In an act of self-immolation, Domenico dies on one of Rome's squares. Before that, however, he gives Gorchakov a candle and orders him to cross an almost dry pool which Gorchakov has lived near. But Gorchakov's task is not at all simple: once lit, this candle must stay lit all the way from one side of the pool to the other. After Domenico is gone Gorchakov tries to cross the pool, but the candle goes out. After several failed attempts, Gorchakov reaches the end of the pool and dies with the candle in his hand.

Writing as Exorcism

The film is clearly about nostalgia: Gorchakov cannot overcome it and, as a result, he dies. Andrei Tarkovsky wrote about the film's topic:

> I wanted to make a film about Russian nostalgia—about that state of mind peculiar to our nation which affects Russians who are far from their native land. I saw this almost as a patriotic duty in my understanding of the concept. I wanted the film to be about the fatal attachment of Russians to their national roots, their past, their culture, their native places, their families and friends; an attachment which they carry with them all their lives, regardless of where *destiny* may fling them. *Russians are seldom able to adapt easily, to come to terms with a new way of life* [emphasis added].[7]

The *destiny* of Gorchakov is thus his inability to adapt to his new life, and that is why he is doomed to die. The only person who unites him with the new reality is Domenico, a "grotesque lunatic," as Tarkovsky himself called him. Why exactly is Domenico this person?

For Russians—traditionally—a madman is often a messenger of some kind of secret wisdom. In his earlier films *Andrei Rublev* (1966) and *Stalker* (1979), Tarkovsky expressed the same opinion: a holy fool in the former and an almost insane guide—the stalker—in the latter are both, so to speak, *sacred*. Domenico plays their role in *Nostalgia*. As Tarkovsky put it, "Gorchakov is affected by the *total integrity, almost holiness,* of the man and his action [emphasis added]."[8] Domenico is *whole,* and he is a holy man. That is why he insists on the need for a *united* world, and that is why—for Gorchakov—he unites him with the world that is, according to their shared belief, fragmented.

Because—for Gorchakov—Domenico is a holy man, almost a saint, he *believes* in his candle as he might believe in a miracle-working icon: he is convinced that if he crosses the pool in the right way something will *change* in his life. Instead, life is changed by death. The self-immolation of Domenico and the candle of Gorchakov form a "rhyming pair" in the film. And here we can trace what reflects Tarkovsky's own psychological dominant.

Speaking about the nostalgia of his hero, Tarkovsky openly admitted that the feeling was in fact his own:

> I myself went through something similar when I had been away from home for some time: *my encounter with another world and another culture and the beginning of an attachment to them had set up an irritation, barely perceptible but incurable—rather like unrequited love,* like a symptom of the hopelessness of trying to grasp what is boundless, or unite what cannot be joined; a reminder of how finite, how curtailed, our experience on earth must be; like a warning sign of the limitations which predetermine your life, *imposed not*

Exorcism and "the Extra" in the Text

by outward circumstances (those would be easy enough to deal with!) but by your inner 'taboo' . . . [emphasis added].⁹

If—from Tarkovsky's words—we try to conclude what kind of a dominant this might be, we will most surely say: Tarkovsky is afraid of a new world around, he is already attached to it but fears that he—like his hero—will not be able to become part of it. His nostalgia is a fear of not being included.

A second self-admission of Tarkovsky leads us to what I call his personal code in the film. He says:

I am always *lost in admiration* for those mediaeval Japanese artists who worked in the court of their overlord until they had achieved recognition and founded a school, and then, at the peak of their fame, *would change their entire lives by going off to a new place to start working again under a different name and in another style.* . . . It is a phenomenon that has always stirred my imagination, perhaps because *I myself am quite incapable of making any change* in the logic of my life . . . [emphasis added].¹⁰

Tarkovsky is clear: he would *like* to change his life, but is not sure how to do so. This ambiguous feeling—of a new world, which he *admires* and *fears* because of the possible nostalgia—finds its final shape in the finale of the film. The very last shot in it is, probably, one of the best: a Russian house, sort of a hut, is placed inside the Western cathedral. Tarkovsky himself explains it this way:

I would concede that the final shot of *Nostalgia* has an element of metaphor, when I bring the Russian house inside the Italian cathedral which *smacks of literariness:* a model of the hero's state, of the division within him which prevents him from living as he has up till now. Or perhaps, on the contrary, it is his new wholeness in which the Tuscan hills and the Russian countryside come together indissolubly; *he is conscious of them as inherently his own, merged into his being and his blood, but at the same time reality is enjoining him to separate these things by returning to Russia* [emphasis added].¹¹

Indeed, this image is very literarily oriented, and Tarkovsky is conscious of this. But how? What is literary in it? In his explanation, Tarkovsky seems to want to disorient the audience by providing it with no real key to this otherwise beautiful shot. He tries to divert its attention from asking this "why?"— why exactly the *house?* why exactly the *cathedral?*—and thus explains it in a nebulous way. Tarkovsky's reasons for doing this can be understood: he hated questions of the "why" type. He even said at one point: ". . . it seems that the cinema-goer has so lost the capacity simply to surrender to an immediate, emotional aesthetic impression, that he instantly has to check himself, and ask: 'Why? What for? What's the point?'"[12]

In some respect, Tarkovsky is right: not everything—especially a metaphor—can be explained. At the same time, his words sound like: don't touch it! It is too *personal*. Still, the audience is within its rights to ask its "why." If—as Tarkovsky admits—this is a metaphor, and not just a visual but a literary one, then there can be a literary explanation for why he put precisely a house into a cathedral.

Here is a possible explanation. Gorchakov—we remember—is a Russian poet. Tarkovsky's father, Arseny (1907–89), was one of the most important Russian poets of the second part of the century. Andrei grew up surrounded by poetry. Moreover, Andrei Tarkovsky used his father's poems in three of his films: *The Mirror, Stalker*, and *Nostalgia*. In *Nostalgia*, Gorchakov reads Arseny Tarkovsky's poems as his own.

The film is about nostalgia, and thus it is about some painful parting with the past: with the family, too. Also, it is about joining the present. Both things—past and present—Tarkovsky unites in a poetic image, constructed linguistically. In Russian, "house" is *dom;* a cathedral of the type shown in the film is *domskii sobor;* both are related to the same root that produces the Italian *duomo* and English "dome." In Russian, both things—house and cathedral—are *already* parts of each other. And let us not forget that the hero who *unites* the otherwise different realities in the film and makes them *whole* is *Domenico*. Indeed, Tarkovsky's final metaphor totally derives from the sound of his language!

In his explanation of this metaphor Tarkovsky is, so to speak, half honest. He says that it comes from literature but does not mention how. He does not want us to see his *concealed* parting from the past and joining the present. (He had not yet decided to stay in Italy forever, and the film was shot in order to be shown in the USSR.) In the film, Tarkovsky exorcises his own fears of this parting in order to start a new life. He kills his hero, Gorchakov, because he wants to get rid of the past, of the possible nostalgia. (A similar device will be described in chapter 2.) He uses the sound of the Russian *language* when creating a *visual* image—a most unusual thing!—because he most probably fears that he will lose it in a foreign milieu.

This scene demonstrates well the way in which a given image can do double duty as both an aesthetic signifier for the audience of a work of art and as an author's personal code. For the film's viewer, the scene of a Russian house placed inside an Italian cathedral is a wholly successful aesthetic illustration of the theme of unification of seemingly disparate elements, something in the manner of a cinematic *matreshka* doll. That this same scene might have strong coded personal resonance for Tarkovsky is thus irrelevant to the viewer, whose aesthetic sense is fully satisfied by what is offered within the film's code.

Soon after Gorchakov is gone and the exorcism is thus over, Tarkovsky finally decides to stay abroad. He believes that he has already displayed the scenario of his own death—from nostalgia. Although Tarkovsky believes in destiny and uses the concept quite frequently in his essay on *Nostalgia*, although he thinks that it cannot be changed, he plays with it over the head of Gorchakov, whom he kills—the same "trick" will be discussed in chapter 2—and thus attempts to follow the track of a Japanese artist.

In Tarkovsky-the-exorcist, it is also important that he is a poet because he approaches even the art of film through poetry.

FINAL NOTES ON THE TERM

Son-father. Harold Bloom in his *Anxiety of Influence* writes: "Oedipus, *blind*, was on the path to oracular godhood, and the strong poets have followed him by transforming their *blindness* towards their precursors into the revisionary insights of their own work. . . . Battle between strong equals, father and son as mighty opposites, Laius and Oedipus at the crossroads . . . That even the strongest poets are subject to influences not poetical is obvious even to me, but again my concern is only *with the poet in a poet,* or the aboriginal poetic self [emphases, except for the last one, added]."[13]

It is obvious even to me that influences, poetical and not, are sometimes blind. It is also clear that one author sometimes struggles with another in order to become "aboriginal." (An example of this sort will be discussed in chapter 2.)

The battles described in this book are combats against many secret personal fears and struggles for many secret wishes. The authors are aware of them and are in control of this knowledge. They are, so to speak, fully *sighted*, but they want us to remain *blind*. My task here is to try to reveal their secrets. However, as Igor Smirnov has put it, "a scholar's mistakes in this case are by no means excluded."

Chapter Two

Two Superstitious Men

> Предрассудок! он обломок
> Древней равды. Храм упал;
> А руин его потомок
> Языка не разгадал.
>
> Prejudice! it is a fragment
> of ancient truth. The temple collapsed;
> but the successors could not solve
> the language of its ruins.
> —Evgeny Baratynsky (1841)

I

In all of Russian culture one could probably not find anyone as openly superstitious as Alexander Pushkin. The same can be said of many of his characters: heroes and heroines read fortune-telling books, see prophetic dreams, and are full of forebodings. Of course, the issue of superstitions and prophesying, divination, and prejudices was one of the most popular in Pushkin's era. It becomes a theme and the engine of the plot in Zhukovsky's celebrated ballad "Svetlana" (1813):

> Раз в крещенский вечерок
>   Девушки гадали:
> За ворота башмачок,
>   Сняв с ноги, бросали . . .
> Вот красавица одна;
>   К зеркалу садится;
> С тайной робостью она
>   В зеркало глядится;
> Темно в зеркале; кругом

Two Superstitious Men

> Мертвое молчанье;
> Свечка трепетным огнем
> Чуть льет сиянье . . .[1]

> Once on Epiphany eve
>   the maidens were telling their fortunes;
> having taken off a shoe,
>   they threw it over the gate . . .
> Now one beauty is finally alone;
>   she sits before the mirror;
> with secret shyness she
>   looks into the mirror;
> it is dark there; all around
>   dead silence reigns;
> the candle, with its trembling fire,
>   barely sheds a light . . .

Later, in *Eugene Onegin,* Pushkin would use Svetlana's dream and divination as models for Tatyana's.

The issue of superstition stood in for the general early nineteenth-century interest in folk culture. It characterized attempts to get back to roots in order to create a bridge between the ancient and modern world, typical for European Romanticism. At the same time, this interest was not merely window dressing; rather it reflected a metaphysical anxiety of the Romantic literati. The fact that the concern was widespread is somewhat ironically pictured in *Eugene Onegin,* in which two very apposite "specimens" of the Romantic generation, Onegin and Lensky, nevertheless find it a mutually stimulating topic to discuss:

> Between them, every topic started
> reflection or provoked dispute:
> treaties of nations long departed,
> and good and ill, and learning's fruit,
> *the prejudices of the ages,*
> *the secrets of the grave, the pages*
> *of fate, and life,* each in its turn
> became their scrutiny's concern.
> —chapter 2, stanza XVI; emphasis added[2]

Pushkin's slightly ironic approach to the issue in his novel does not at all cancel its serious side. Thus, Evgeny Baratynsky, who held the same aesthetic views as Pushkin and was one of the most philosophically minded poets of the

Writing as Exorcism

generation, tried, as can be seen from the epigraph, to interpret ancient beliefs as some secret code, which nature had given humans in the hope that one day they would break it and obtain full knowledge. Baratynsky wrote another poem on this topic, "The Omens" ("Primety"), in 1839, two years after Pushkin's death. Here, he bitterly sums up the experience of his generation (and their failure to break the code) and speaks of a new generation—that of Lermontov, let us say—the cool pragmatists, who do not trust anything but themselves and only believe in what they see with their own eyes:

> Пока человек естества не пытал
>   Горнилом, весами и мерой,
> Но детски вещаньям природы внимал,
>   Ловил ее знаменья с верой;
> Покуда природу любил он, она
>   Любовью ему отвечала,
> О нем дружелюбной заботы полна,
>   Язык для него обретала. . . .
> Но, чувство презрев, он доверил уму;
>   Вдался в суету изысканий . . .
> И сердце природы закрылось ему,
>   И нет на земле прорицаний . . .[3]

> Before man started testing nature
>   with hearth, weights and ruler,
> but like a child listened to its prophesying,
>   he caught its signs through faith;
> As long as he was in love with nature, it
>   answered him with the same love,
> and took friendly care of him,
>   designed for him a language. . . .
> But he scorned his senses and started trusting his reason;
>   fell into the vanity of research . . .
> And the heart of nature became closed to him,
>   and there are no soothsayings on the earth.

Although the tones used by the two major Russian Romantic poets on the topic were different—Baratynsky was always much gloomier—the ironic pitch of Pushkin's voice nevertheless reflected his human concerns, too. For now, let us call this kind of concern "an exorcism of superstitions with irony." And, following the principles of Pushkin's novel, let us reconcile ourselves, in regard to the discussion of this concern, to digressions that are sometimes longer and more important than the main story. These digressions may at first seem a bit boring because they follow the principle of the catalogue, but they are necessary to illustrate that however ironically he may have treated superstitions in his work, in his own life Pushkin thought and felt seriously about them.

DIGRESSION 1: A CATALOGUE OF PUSHKIN'S SUPERSTITIONS

Among the many objects of Pushkin's superstition the most acclaimed happens to be . . . a hare. The tale of the one that crossed Pushkin's path on his way to Petersburg on the eve of the Decembrist uprising of 1825 and "returned" him to his estate, thereby preventing Pushkin from joining the revolutionaries on the Senate Square, is indeed famous. M. Pogodin tells it this way:

> Pushkin had wanted to see his Petersburg friends for a long time. . . . So then, Pushkin orders his carriage prepared and tells his servant to be ready to go with him to Petersburg, but first he has to say good-bye to his neighbors, the ladies in Trigorskoe. However, on his way to Trigorskoe a hare crosses his path; on the way back to Mikhailovskoe—another hare! In a lather, Pushkin returns home; he is told that the servant, who had been ready to go, had suddenly gotten a fever. He calls for another servant. Finally, the carriage is prepared, they start moving from the porch. Lo and behold! at the gate they meet a priest who was coming to say good-bye to the departing landowner. All these meetings are too much for the superstitious Pushkin; he returns home from the gate and stays on his estate.[4]

To this, Prince Viazemsky adds: "Pogodin told about Pushkin's planned visit to Petersburg incognito in December 1825 correctly. I heard the same from Pushkin himself. However, as far as I remember, there were not two hares but only one. Otherwise, it is very true that he would have gotten into the cauldron of the uprising at Ryleev's that night, between the 13th and the 14th."[5]

Why exactly did a priest and a hare prevent Pushkin from going to Petersburg? According to a common Russian superstition seeing a priest at the beginning of a journey is a bad sign.[6] A hare is a bad omen in both English and Russian folk cultures. In Russia, the collective fear of seeing a jumping hare is imprinted in the proverb, "When a hare crosses the road it brings lots of trouble."[7] In *Eugene Onegin*, we read, once again, about Tatyana (stanza VI):

> And if she happened anywhere
> to meet a black monk, or if crossing
> her path a hare in headlong flight
> ran through the fields, sheer panic fright
> would leave her dithering and tossing.

Thus, Tatyana reacted exactly the way her creator did! For us, it is less important to know whether Pushkin used, or even invented, the entire hare accident as an excuse to stay away from Petersburg than to observe that at various times hares continued to lead him astray. Another description of a villainous jumper belongs to E. Novosiltseva, and the year she describes is 1830:

> The estate where Pushkin lived in Nizhnii [Novgorod] was a few miles from Apraksino village that belonged to the Novosiltsev family. Pushkin liked them a lot, especially the mistress of the house, a very kind and pleasant old lady. She very often rebuked him for being superstitious, a feature that indeed reached an unbelievable point in his character. Lady Novosiltsev was celebrating her name day, and Pushkin had promised to visit for a dinner; people were waiting for him for far too long and finally decided to start without him. Champagne had been already served, when he appeared, approached the one whose name-day it was and knelt before her. "Natalia Alexeevna," he said, "don't be mad at me: I had already left my home and was near your place when this damned hare crossed my way. You know I am a holy-fool: I returned home and left my carriage; but then I took it out again and came to you in order to have my ears boxed ["chtoby Vy menia vydrali za ushi"]."[8]

Hares never seemed to stop nagging our hero. Another episode took place in 1834. The overseer of Pushkin's estate, Boldino, recounted that Pushkin had once invited a servant for a night ride to his favorite wood, and "they had just passed the barn when a hare suddenly appeared before them and crossed their path. Pushkin immediately returned home."[9] Finally, we have Pushkin's own affirmation of his strange relationship with this unpredictable creature. In 1833, he wrote to his wife: "I am once again in Simbirsk. Three days ago, I left at night and was on my way to Orenburg. The very moment I reached the main road, a hare crossed before me. . . . On our way back I fell asleep; I wake up in the morning—we didn't make even five miles. . . . The Devil only knows how God helped us, but we are finally back in Simbirsk. I would have given anything to become a borzoi—I would sure have found that hare."[10]

Interestingly enough, Pushkin believed not only in tried-and-true bad omens, such as hares or black monks, but in many other things that only he interpreted as bad auguries. Thus, right before his marriage in 1831, Pushkin visited his favorite gypsy singer, Tania, who performed a song for him:

> Oh, my dear mother, why is that dust in the fields?
> Ma'am, why is that dust?
> The horses got up. But whose are these horses, whose are they?
> The horses of Alexander Sergeevich . . .

"I am singing this song," she confessed later, "and feel so sad, and I convey this feeling with all my voice . . . And suddenly I hear: Pushkin has started to cry out loud . . . Pavel [Nashchokin] rushed to him: 'What's the matter with you, what's the matter, Pushkin?'—'Ah,' he says, 'this song of hers turned all my insides out, it bodes me no good but a big-big loss!' After this, he didn't stay long; left without saying good-bye."[11]

Furthermore, at his own wedding Pushkin experienced a whole series of bad omens, which he took rather fatalistically. "During the ceremony," describes an anonymous witness, "Pushkin accidentally brushed against a lectern and pushed over a crucifix; people say that when the rings were exchanged one of them fell on the floor . . . The poet's countenance changed and he whispered to one of those present: 'tous les mauvais augures!'" "During the wedding ceremony," claims another witness, Princess Dolgorukov, "a cross and a Bible fell down from a lectern when the newly-weds were going around it. Pushkin went totally pale. Then, his candle went out. 'Tous les mauvais augures,' said Pushkin."[12] Given his nature, the poet had good reason to be worried. As a Russian popular belief insists, "already during a wedding ceremony people can judge from the wedding candles which of the parties to a marriage will die first. The one whose wedding candle goes out first will die before the other one."[13]

However, it would not be fair to say that Pushkin's mind was preoccupied only with bad omens. He believed in good ones, too, albeit in a surprising minority of cases. Thus, already after his marriage and perhaps trying to challenge the bad omens of his wedding with at least a single favorable one, Pushkin writes to his friend Nashchokin: "At your place, I dropped a silver coin [*serebrianuiu kopeechku*]. If you find it, send it to me. You don't believe in their good luck but I do."[14]

As we have seen, Pushkin fully shared a superstitious nature with his character Tatyana. However, the question we still want to ask is whether this feature of Pushkin's personality was stamped in works besides *Eugene Onegin*. In order to show not the *overt*, as in his novel and in the general line of life, but the *encoded* superstitious Pushkin, we will turn to the most mysterious and thus "problematic" of his prose works, *The Queen of Spades*.

Writing as Exorcism

APPROACH TO *THE QUEEN OF SPADES* 1: PUSHKIN'S CARD PASSION

> Сын время, случая, судьбины
> Иль недоведомой причины,
> Бог сильный, резвый, добрый, злой! . . .
> В те дни, как все везде в разгулье:
> Политика и правосудье,
> Ум, совесть, и закон святой,
> И логика пиры пируют,
> На карты ставят век златой,
> Судьбами смертных пунтируют,
> Вселенну в трателево гнут . . .

> Son of a time, of chance, of fate
> or of not fully known purpose,
> mighty, playful, kind, malicious God! . . .
> In those days, everywhere everything is wild:
> politics and justice,
> mind, conscience, and sacred law,
> and logic are feasting,
> staking on cards a golden age,
> punting with human destinies,
> multiplying their stakes by thirty [against]
>   the universe. . . .
> —Gavriil Derzhavin, "On Luck"
>   ("Na schastie," 1789)[15]

Derzhavin's verses, although written in the eighteenth century and about it, are also appropriate for Pushkin's era: "punting with human destinies" and thus competing with one's own luck, that capricious god, as Derzhavin called it, becomes a leitmotif of the early nineteenth-century way of thinking and, consequently, art. As Mikhail Gorlin, an émigré poet and scholar, once wittily put it:

> There is no other literature but Russian in which people play cards with such abandon, and that is why the history of gambling and games of chance can be exactly traced in literary texts. In Pushkin's era games of chance are in the foreground. In reality and in literature people play faro furiously. This game is amazing in its simplicity; a four-year-old kid can learn it with the same success as some experienced and mature card-player. A banker takes the deck

and starts placing cards on his two sides. Before that, players put a sum of money on this or that card. If the card falls to banker's left, he takes the stake; if to his right—he pays a player twice as much. *The Queen of Spades* is built up entirely on this uncomplicated combination.[16]

Though the game of faro, which is a focus of *The Queen of Spades,* is indeed easy, its broader meaning is rather intricate. The significance of faro as a game with a strong metaphysical bias was shown in detail by Iurii Lotman in his already classic study, "*The Queen of Spades* and the Theme of Cards and the Card Game in Russian Literature of the Beginning of the Nineteenth Century." Lotman writes:

> The situation in faro is, first of all, the situation of a duel: modeled as a conflict of its two opponents. However, the very essence of this model becomes their inequality: the punter—the one who wants to win all, though he risks losing everything—behaves like a person who has to make some important decisions without having any substantive information; he can either act at random or make assumptions trying to deduce some statistical regularities (it is known that in Pushkin's library there were books on the theory of probability; perhaps, they were connected to his attempts to find the best possible strategy for himself as a punter). On the contrary, the banker has no strategy at all. Moreover, a person who places the cards does not himself know which side a card will fall on. He is, so to speak, a dummy in the hands of the Unknown Factors behind his back. In itself, this model already hid a certain interpretation of life conflicts. The game had become a clash with a mighty and irrational power, very often taken as demonic. . . .[17]

In the plot of *The Queen of Spades,* the demonic and the esoteric parts of the game play a featured role. Hermann, the story's protagonist who never gambles because of his frugality, is told at a card party a legend of how an old countess, the grandmother of one of the participants, had been given in her youth a secret of three cards that infallibly win. Hermann becomes obsessed with the idea of these three winning cards, finds his way to the countess's house—having faked a liaison with the countess's ward, Lizaveta—and literally scares her to death. After the funeral, the countess's ghost appears before Hermann and tells him the names of the three cards that are supposed to win him a fortune. Hermann starts gambling; he wins on two cards, but then loses everything on the third. Unable to handle this loss, Hermann goes mad.

Already on the level of plot, *The Queen of Spades* touches upon two momentous topics: the passion for gambling (Hermann) and gambling with the unknown (the three mysterious cards from the other world). What is more, the former was characteristic of Pushkin himself: he was a true card addict. Thus, A. Vul'f writes:

> No other game gives us so many vivacious and various emotions as cards, because even at the time when you are most unlucky you always hope to get on, or, simply, because in even the greatest loss there is always the hope, the probability of a win. This I have heard from the passionate players; for example, from Pushkin (the poet) . . . Pushkin once justly told me, that the passion for games of chance is the strongest of all passions.[18]

Indeed, Pushkin's passion for cards outweighed even his passion for women. Prince Viazemsky, for example, recalls:

> Pushkin, in the time of his stay in Southern Russia, once rode a couple hundred miles away to a ball where he hoped to meet the object of his love. Having arrived in the city, he—before the ball—sat down to punt and played all night long until the late morning, thus losing all his money, and the ball, and his love.[19]

Another friend of Pushkin's, P. Bartenev, also remembered that "Pushkin dedicated a large part of his time to cards. . . . Any quick change, any type of boldness was to his liking; he took to games of chance and all his life after that could not escape this passion."[20] It is noteworthy that the word "passion" is frequently used when people tell us about Pushkin's relationship with cards. "It was known," adds K. Polevoi, "that he usually played for big stakes, often losing all his money. It grieved me greatly to see this extraordinary man burning with such a coarse and dull passion."[21]

The testimonies regarding Pushkin's passion for cards are endless. What is more important, however, is that Pushkin himself treated his passion as part and parcel of his superstitious nature. Anna Kern recalled that he "loved cards very much and said that they were his only affection. Like all players, he was superstitious, and once, when I asked him for money for some poor family, he gave me his last fifty roubles and said: 'You are lucky that I lost yesterday.'"[22]

Furthermore, the function of cards, as Iurii Lotman explains, is marked by a double nature: "On the one hand, cards are the *game*, that is, they are a kind of conflict situation. . . . On the other hand, cards are used in fortune-telling. There, different functions of cards become active: both the prognosticating and programming ones."[23] It seems that all these different functions of cards were taken equally seriously by Pushkin along with the "prejudices of the ages" (*"predrassudki vekovye"*). Moreover, in their "second" function cards brought many strange incidents into Pushkin's life, and they started immediately after his visit to the famous Petersburg fortune-teller Madame Kirchhof.

DIGRESSION 2: A FORTUNE-TELLER

"Charlotta Fedorovna Kirchhof, a widow, people said, of a pastor, had arrived in Petersburg in the week of Palm Sunday, 1818.... A tall old woman, about sixty years old, she scarcely recalled a sorceress. Rather, her fresh face suggested the old women of Rembrandt.... A black woollen dress and a similar shawl with a narrow Turkish hem were her permanent attire.... At her suite, Kirchhof was visited mainly by men, the young and aged, not only by civilians but guardsmen as well. Many came to her chuckling, but left sober and gloomy; her prophecies were not believed, people called them nonsense and lies—however, all this nonsense had been stamped in their memory, and her prophecy was like a sword of Damocles, which they voluntarily hung over their own heads," wrote the historian and novelist P. Karatygin.[24] Although his description of a German fortune-teller appears in a work of fiction and her given names and the date of her arrival to Russia's capital are inaccurate—Aleksandra Fillipovna Kirchhof actually came to Russia at the very beginning of the 1810s—her role in Petersburg society of the teens and twenties is not at all overstated: Kirchhof's services were used even by the Emperor Alexander I. Before the war with Napoleon he visited her (incognito, of course), was "unveiled" by the lady and then told that "in the beginning" he would "face a disaster," but afterward he would "overcome it." "Your future is brilliant," she promised Alexander I.[25]

Another Alexander—Pushkin—visited her, most likely in 1819.[26] He was then nineteen years old. A confidant of Pushkin's, Sergei Sobolevsky, described the meeting as follows:

> I often heard directly from him about this event; he loved telling it in response to the jokes provoked by his belief in various omens. Moreover, in my presence he told this story many times to those who had been to the fortune-teller themselves.... Her prophecy [to Pushkin] was, that, first, he would soon get money; second, that he would unexpectedly get an offer; third, that he would become famous and an idol for his compatriots; fourth, that he would twice go into exile; finally, that he would live long if in the thirty-seventh year of his life he could avoid some disaster brought to him either by a white horse, by blond hair, or by a white man (weisser Ross, weisser Kopf, weisser Mensch). Those he was to avoid. The first prophecy, about money, came true the same evening: Pushkin, when he returned home, found an absolutely surprising letter from a friend from the Lycee, who informed Pushkin that a card debt about which

Pushkin had forgotten had been sent to him. . . . Not less surprising was also a proposition from Alexei Fedorovich Orlov, who, a few days later, called to him in the theater and . . . offered him a place in the cavalry-guards.[27]

Another acquaintance of Pushkin's, Pavel Mansurov, adds to this: "Kirchhof's prophecies had a huge impact on Pushkin, especially in the beginning, but soon, it seemed to us, they were completely blotted out of his memory. However, when some of us reminded him of them, it became clear that he did not like this; in every way possible he tried to change the subject, and if he could not succeed he started guffawing sooner than others, though for all who knew him well it was obvious that his guffaw was forced, and this only made us stop even hinting at what had happened."[28]

Apparently, Pushkin told this story to many people. One of those, a lady, recalled it as follows:

"You, perhaps, will find it amazing," again started Pushkin, "that I believe in a good deal of the unbelievable and incomprehensible; I was forced to become so superstitious by one event. With N. Vsevolozhsky, I was once walking on Nevsky Prospect and, playing pranks, we dropped in to a woman who told fortunes by looking at coffee grounds. We asked her to tell our fortunes and, without telling about the past, foresee our future. "'You,' she told me, 'will meet your old acquaintance one of these days, and he will offer you a great position; then, also soon, you will get some unexpected money by mail; and third, I must tell you, your death will be unnatural.' Of course, I forgot about the fortune-teller and her prophecies the same day. However, two weeks later, and again on Nevsky, I indeed met an old friend, who had been an employee of the Grand Prince Konstantin Mikhailovich in Warsaw and was now working in Petersburg; he started offering me and persuading to take his place in Warsaw, assuring me that the Prince himself wanted this. This was the first time after the divination that I recollected the fortune-teller. In just a few days I indeed got a letter with money in it; and how could have I expected that? This money was sent by my schoolmate from the Lycee, with whom I had played cards many years before and won. He had gotten an inheritance from his late father and sent me his debt which I not only had not expected but had completely forgotten about. Now, the third prophecy should come true, and I am absolutely sure about it." The superstition of such an educated man amused me then very much.[29]

Although the details in two versions of the prophecies obtained by Pushkin and their after-effects vary, one can nevertheless conclude that he did accept them in a straightforward manner, not much differently from how he treated numerous folk beliefs.

Two Superstitious Men

From 1819 on, white horses and blond men became Pushkin's constant fixations. Thus, in 1827, when courting Ekaterina Ushakova, according to a member of the Ushakov family, he often came to their house "riding a horse." "If this horse happened to be a white one, he always recalled the words of some famous Petersburg fortune-teller . . . that he would die either from a white horse or a blond man—because of his wife." "Apropos," says the same author of memoirs, "Pushkin said that when he had returned from exile and saw the Emperor Nicholas I he thought; 'Is this the blond man on whom my fate depends?'"[30]

In the same year, Pushkin wrote an unexpectedly malicious epigram on the poet A. Muravev, whom he had favored before and who had unintentionally broken the hand of a statue of Apollo during some society ball. "He," claimed Muravev, "did not understand my exculpatory poem written on the statue's pedestal and decided that I had called myself a rival of Apollo."[31] However, Pushkin might have had another reason for getting enraged that relates to his superstitions. We find evidence of exactly this motive in the memoirs of M. Pogodin. He remembered meeting Pushkin a few days after the epigram on Muravev had been published. "'What if I pay for the epigram with my life.'—'Why?'—'I was given a prophecy that I will die either from a white man or a white horse. Muravev can challenge me, and he is not only a white man but a horse's ass as well.'"[32] Pushkin, of course, tried to laugh here, but the fact that he constantly spoke about (and remembered!) Kirchhof's prophecy is more significant. The case of Pushkin's epigram puzzled Muravev, and it was not until some years later that Sobolevsky opened his eyes to the reasons for Pushkin's impulsiveness: "Pushkin had always had a passion for finding out his future from various fortune-tellers. One of them told him that he has to avoid a tall blond young man, from whom his death would come. Pushkin is very superstitious, and that is why when chance brings him together with a man who has all these features, he starts to think: is not precisely he that homme-fatal? He even tries to irritate him in order to tempt his fate as soon as possible."[33]

Surprisingly enough, all the references to Pushkin's fixation on Kirchhof's prophecies somehow vanish from the memoirs describing his life after his marriage, even if Pushkin remembered (and we know) that "he would die either from a white horse or a blond man—*because of his wife* [emphasis added]." Moreover, Pushkin seems not to have been alerted even by the appearance of d'Antès, his future murderer, in his life. This is despite the fact, as recalls one of Pushkin's contemporaries, that d'Antès "was a young man, neither handsome nor ugly, rather tall, somehow clumsy, *blond, with a small fair-haired mustache* [emphasis added]."[34] Had Pushkin ceased to be superstitious? We shall see later. But one of the reasons why he might have, I believe, lies precisely behind *The Queen of Spades*.

APPROACH TO *THE QUEEN OF SPADES* 2: "THREE CARDS, THREE CARDS, THREE CARDS . . ."

In Peter Tchaikovsky's opera, the words "three cards, three cards, three cards" are the refrain of Hermann's famous aria. Indeed, the number of mysterious cards, three, and the rank of each of them—three, seven, and ace—make them the pivot of an otherwise unpretentious story about a greedy man. Because of this feature, efforts to read *The Queen of Spades* as a densely coded text, connected with its numerology, have become popular among common readers and curious scholars alike. This "trend" had already begun in Pushkin's time. In 1834, Pushkin wrote in his *Diary:* "My *Queen of Spades* is the latest fashion—players punt on the three, the seven, and the ace. At court, people have found a resemblance between the old Countess and Princess Nat. Petr. Golitsyna, and, it seems to me, they are not offended. Following my advice, Gogol started a history of Russian criticism."[35] I keep the entire passage together, with all the "gossip" and especially the reference to Gogol, in order to demonstrate how flippant Pushkin was about his own numbers, in stark contrast to the seriousness with which readers and critics have taken them. In the story, their portrayal is even more openly ironic:

> The three, the seven, and the ace soon overshadowed the image of the dead old woman in Hermann's mind. Three, seven, ace—the threesome haunted him and was perpetually on his lips. Seeing a young girl, he would say, "How shapely! Just like a three of hearts." If anybody asked him what time it was, he would answer, "Five to the seven." Every portly man reminded him of an ace. The three, the seven, and the ace hounded him even in his dreams, taking on every imaginable form: the three blossomed before him like a great luxuriant flower; the seven appeared as a Gothic gate; and the ace assumed the shape of an enormous spider.[36]

Is Pushkin's story just a joke then? The scholars who understand the story as a coded text disagree, of course, and try their best: in the cards' numbers they have even found Masonic allusions.[37] However, as Iurii Lotman wisely put it:

> Speaking about works dedicated to numerical symbolism in *The Queen of Spades*, I have to warn against enthusiasm for such easy rapprochements. It is important to remember that numerical symbolism per se is one of the most universal in world culture and is able to manifest itself on unlimited material.[38]

If the numerology in Pushkin is a kind of practical joke, it is difficult to disagree with Caryl Emerson:

... I would suggest that the codes we get in this story were designed by Pushkin *not* to build any single unified structure or to solve any single puzzle.... The mysteries in *The Queen of Spades* are not really solvable by a single code—as we would expect, say, in a good detective story. And yet the evidence for crackable codes is so overwhelming in *The Queen of Spades* that we, along with Hermann, are almost foisted into the search. This passion on the part of the reader to explain the whole by a single key might well be the real target of Pushkin's parody.[39]

Long ago Boris Eichenbaum pointed out that in *The Queen of Spades* we have a "lowering of the heroic and 'demonic' topic to the level of the German Hermann, that is, almost its parody."[40] If Pushkin's story *is* a parody, or a mystification, then the secret of the three cards as the story's code simply dies away and there is no sense in asking the question what they *mean*.

However, we might still have a few "whys" to ask Pushkin's text. Why, for example, does Hermann win on the three and then on the seven and finally—quite unexpectedly—fail on the ace? Why does exactly the ace, and not the three or the seven, become his unlucky card, although it was given to him from the same source as the other two? Why does exactly the queen of spades come out instead of the ace? Or does Hermann simply make a mistake and select the queen instead of the winning ace? (Recall, Hermann loses not because the ace does not appear, but rather because when he shows his card his stake turns out to be on the queen of spades rather than the ace.) Does this happen just because of the epigraph to the story—"the queen of spades signifies secret ill-will"? And why does she signify exactly that? In order to offer my version not of what those cards *mean* for/in the story but of why exactly these three are *employed* in it, I have to return once again to Pushkin's biography and his superstitious nature.

DIGRESSION 3: GOGOL, PUSHKIN, HERMANN

Is it possible that Pushkin simultaneously keeps *The Queen of Spades* as a very personal thing, for himself, and as quite another thing for a public audience? Is this not similar to Pushkin's habit of laughing—before others begin—at what he otherwise takes very seriously? It also fits with the poet's tendency to treat simultaneously the same material seriously and parodically, as, for example, the famous contrast between his poem "I recall a marvellous moment" dedicated to Anna Kern and his obscene letter referring to the same event.[41]

Let us start with the first possible personal code in *The Queen of Spades*. From the work's "conclusion" we know that "Hermann has lost his mind. He is at the Obukhov Hospital, ward number 17; he doesn't answer

Writing as Exorcism

questions, just keeps muttering with uncommon rapidity, "three, seven, ace! Three, seven, queen!"[42]

The Queen of Spades was written in 1834. In 1833, Pushkin wrote *The Bronze Horseman* in which the protagonist, "poor Evgeny," goes mad. In the same year Pushkin wrote a poem that is simultaneously a prayer and a cry, "Please, God, do not let me go mad . . ." ("Ne dai mne Bog soiti s uma . . ."). In January 1834, the year of our story, Pushkin, by the tsar's decree, became a gentleman of the bedchamber *(kamer-iunker)*. "This made him insane," writes one of Pushkin's contemporaries.[43] "I cannot repeat here everything that the incensed poet, foaming at the mouth, said about this appointment."[44] From this time on, Count Grabbe recalled, "the passionate, inspired Pushkin was no more. Some kind of sadness was on his face."[45] In 1835, Pushkin's anxiety got worse. He wrote a strange poem, "A Pilgrim" ("Strannik"), in which the motifs found in the "on madness" poem of 1833 only become more prominent. The poem starts:

> Однажды, странствуя среди долины дикой,
> Незапно был объят я скорбию великой
> И тяжким бременем подавлен и согбен.
> Как тот, кто на суде в убийстве уличен.
> Потупя голову, в тоске ломая руки,
> Я в воплях изливал души пронзенной муки
> И горько повторял, метаясь как больной:
> "Что делать буду я? что станется со мной?"

> Once wandering in a wild valley
> I was suddenly engulfed by enormous grief,
> weighed down and bent by a heavy burden.
> Like one, who has been found guilty of murder in court.
> Having lowered my head, wringing my hands in anguish,
> I unbosomed the pangs of my pierced soul in howls
> and, tossing like a sick man, I bitterly repeated:
> "What will I do? what will become of me?"

The anxiety of the hero, although adopted from John Bunyan's novel of 1678 to 1684, *Pilgrim's Progress,* looks intensely autobiographical.[46] Especially, the questions addressed to the invisible future, "What will I do? what will become of me?" seem to be about his own destiny. Later in the poem, he returns home and tells his family:

> "О горе, горе нам! Вы, дети, ты, жена!—
> Сказал я,—ведайте: моя душа полна

Two Superstitious Men

Тоской и ужасом; мучительное бремя
Тягчит меня. Идет! уж близко, близко время:
Наш город пламени и ветрам обречен;
Он в угли и золу вдруг будет обращен,
И мы погибнем все, коль не успеем вскоре
Обресть убежище: а где? о горе, горе!"
    Мои домашние в смущение пришли
И здравый ум во мне расстроенным почли. . . .

"Oh, woe, woe to us! You, children, and you, wife!"
I said: "You should know: my soul is full
of anguish and horror; a tormenting burden
lies heavy on me. It's coming! the time is close, close:
our city will be condemned to fire and to the winds;
it will suddenly be turned into coals and ashes,
and we'll all die if we don't soon
find shelter; but where? oh, woe, woe!"
    My family were troubled
and they considered my sane mind disordered. . . .

It is hard to separate the poetic hero's prophesying of coming disaster from what Pushkin himself had been most probably feeling for the three or so years before his mortal duel of 1837. His concern about wife and children (in 1835, he already had two); the symbolic "city," which, of course, is related to life in general; his foreboding of imminent destruction; his attempt to escape from the stifling reality and the impossibility of such an escape (where to go?—to Mikhailovskoe? to Boldino?); the reputation of a "madman," a man with a short temper—all these autobiographical details are featured in the poem. About the last of them, a contemporary wrote: "According to those who watched Pushkin closely, he sometimes felt such an impulsiveness and rush of blood that he had to freshen his head with water, and for this purpose he—in the middle of a lively conversation—suddenly ran out into another room."[47]

In 1835, the year of "A Pilgrim," Pushkin's worries about his wife and children increased constantly. Moreover, they were again connected to his superstitions. "Today I saw the moon on my left and started fretting about you enormously," he wrote to his wife from Mikhailovskoe on September 14.[48] The moon is indeed significant: according to the folk belief, "the new moon over the right shoulder brings luck, over the left means coming disaster."[49] On September 21, he wrote again with concerns about her and their children's financial future: ". . . neither I, nor your aunt are immortal. God knows, what might happen! For now, it is just sadness."[50] Toward the end of September 1835, Pushkin's refrain, "what will happen," becomes even more frequent. "I am losing time and spirit, I waste all the money I earn and see nothing in the future. My father squanders the estate without any pleasure; your family is losing everything. What will happen? Lord knows."[51] The line in the poem, "What will I do? what will happen to me?" definitely reflects Pushkin's own mood. "For inspiration," wrote Pushkin to Pletnev from Mikhailovskoe, "I need peace in my heart, and I am not at all calm."[52] Pushkin's sister Olga asserted at the end of 1835: "Alexander is utterly frustrated: he thinks too much about his household, his children and his wife's wardrobe."[53]

If we try to summarize Pushkin's mood of 1833 to 1835, it would look like this:

1833—fear of madness (*The Bronze Horseman* and "Please, God, do not let me go mad . . .");
1834—*The Queen of Spades*, in which Hermann loses his mind;
1835—"A Pilgrim," uncertainty about the future, fear of being understood as a madman (". . . and they found my sane mind disordered"). Moreover, Pushkin's own words plus his contemporaries' opinions fully confirm the reality of what was stamped in all these literary works.

Madness, Pushkin's major concern during the marked period, is, to my mind, his personal connection to Hermann. His personal connection to the story is as important as his passion for gambling, whose significance for the story we will examine later.

As a person, Pushkin, in the eyes of many, was a complete dichotomy: both very serious and almost always ironic. Even in the utterly depressed period of his life just described, Pushkin continued laughing out loud in the company of other people, particularly those who did not know him well. "How happy must Pushkin be!" the famous artist Briullov said, "He laughs as if he would split his sides!"[54] We do not know whether Pushkin's gaiety was real or assumed. But it is important that the laughing Pushkin seemed downhearted when tête-à-tête with his notebooks and with those close to him.

That is why it seems probable that Hermann, an openly *parodic* figure in *The Queen of Spades,* simultaneously represents the other—so to speak—*serious* side of Pushkin. It is likely that this character takes Pushkin's fears upon himself, or, if we put it another way, Pushkin most probably vents them on his hero when making him first farcical and finally insane. It is also significant that the hero is a German, a foreigner, a stranger. By making Hermann a German, Pushkin seems to distance his hero's madness from himself. He estranges his fears in order not to allow them to come close to his own skin (or brain). In Hermann, the parodic facade of the story, he exorcises what he worries about in himself. At the same time, although he makes *Hermann* a parody of his own fears, Pushkin, I will show later, does not want his *story* to be a parody. Rather, *The Queen of Spades* is his personal and, yes, *coded* battlefield with destiny. Before we come to the discussion of Pushkin's second personal code in the story, allow me just another short digression.

Interestingly enough, we find a very similar situation in Gogol. Chapter 3 will show how Gogol's fear of losing his mind is reflected in "The Nose," in which a nose—believe it or not—*is* a mind. If in Pushkin Hermann loses his mind after the loss on an ace, Gogol's Chichikov in *Dead Souls* also loses his mind, though for a short time, and also after a major loss. Moreover, if Pushkin's Hermann is of German origin, then in Gogol's "Nevsky Prospect" a nose (read: mind) is almost lost (cut off) on the "battlefield" of two Germans, Schiller and Hoffmann.

If we leave aside other points of our writers' intersections as well as the big difference in their characters, the two great contemporaries, Pushkin and Gogol, nevertheless meet at the point where the exorcism of their deepest fears of insanity takes forms of laughter and irony with which they treat their characters.

FINAL APPROACH TO *THE QUEEN OF SPADES*:
THREE CARDS, PUSHKIN, AND D'ANTÈS

We have just seen Pushkin laughing openly at Hermann, being simultaneously very open about his worries and fears in his poems and letters. At the same time, these fears are quite coded within the literary work devoted to that same Hermann. What if, by analogy, the three cards, the openly faked "numerology," are not important for the story but for Pushkin himself? What if we try dealing with them not as some numbers meaningful for the story, in which case if we break their code we understand it better, but rather as something that would be meaningful in the case of Pushkin's own life? That is, as his personal, and *purely* personal, code?

Let us recall: Hermann loses on an ace, because the queen of spades unexpectedly takes its place on the table.

> Hermann stood by the table, ready to punt against the pale, though still smiling, Chekalinskii. Each unsealed a new pack of cards. Chekalinskii shuffled. Hermann picked a card and placed it on the table, covering it with a stack of bank notes. It was like a duel. A profound silence reigned over the gathering.
>
> Chekalinskii started dealing with trembling hands. On his right showed a queen, on his left an ace.
>
> "The ace has won!" said Hermann and turned his card face up.

"Your queen has been murdered," said Chekalinskii affably.

Hermann shuddered: indeed, instead of an ace, the queen of spades lay before him. He could not believe his eyes; he could not fathom how he could possibly have pulled the wrong card.

Suddenly, it seemed to him that the queen of spades had screwed up her eyes and grinned. An extraordinary likeness struck him . . .

"The old woman!" he cried out in terror.[55]

Why does the queen of spades precisely "murder" the ace? Probably, the explanation is that that is how Pushkin himself understood what an ace is. Prince Viazemsky recalls:

In the addenda to the posthumous *Collected Works* of Mickiewicz written in French the following story is told. Pushkin, having met Mickiewicz somewhere in the street, stepped aside and said: "The deuce must step aside! the ace is coming!" To this, Mickiewicz answered at once: "A trump deuce murders even an ace!"[56]

Pushkin's joke is slippery: he calls the great Polish poet Mickiewicz (with whom he was very friendly at the time) "the ace," because the word also denotes not only a card but a person of high quality, while he calls himself "the deuce," a small fish, so to speak. Mickiewicz returns the compliment. In Russian, however, an ace *(tuz)* is a negative euphemism for somebody who wants to be more important than he really is. Pushkin's joke thus is somehow ambivalent: he underlines that "the ace" is not as great as people think and, of course, that he, Pushkin, is not "small" at all. Mickiewicz, naturally, got the point, but generously gave the palm to Pushkin.

Were it not for our story this small anecdote would be insignificant. I chose it in order to show that an ace is not just a *card,* but also an important *person,* generally in a pejorative sense, and that Pushkin played on both meanings. Let us suppose then that the ace in *The Queen of Spades* can be not just a card that lost the game for Hermann, but also some *important man* who lost a duel and was actually "killed" by the queen of spades. The trick here is not that Hermann pulled out the wrong card. To my mind, the trick is that Hermann is not at all important; he is just an ironic, or a parodic, camouflage for the mortal duel that the cards are waging among themselves: the cards and Pushkin, who plays them over the heads of his characters. In other words, Pushkin is playing against himself or, more exactly, against his own future.

So then, some important man, the ace, is killed by the queen of spades. This card is indeed very "human": she even "screws up her eyes and grins." Hermann sees in her the old countess, but the entire situation is absurd and just a continuation of an absurd plot with its three cards from other world. However, it would be so *only* if we try to see the story as a *story*, that is, a piece of Pushkin's literature, but not as his *personal document*. If we accept it as the latter, we might find it quite interesting that the queen of spades screwed up her eyes and grinned *(prishchurilas' i usmekhnulas')*. Were these gestures addressed to Hermann? Or, maybe, rather to the author, in case he is the real player? Let us go even further and presume that the queen of spades was another real person for Pushkin, or an incarnation of this somebody. Moreover, her gestures can be both ironic and benevolent, and even approving, depending on which side, Hermann's or Pushkin's, we perceive them from.

If we take Pushkin's side, we should go back to the story's epigraph: "The queen of spades signifies secret ill-will. *From a recent fortune-telling book.*" From here, we should probably ask, for whom does she signify it? If *The Queen of Spades is* Pushkin's coded personal document, then it means that she does so for Pushkin. The only person in Pushkin's life who would fit in the evil queen's place is, of course, the person who foretold him ill will from his own destiny, that is, the fortune-teller Kirchhof.

Magnifying Glass 1

Sergei Sobolevsky wrote: "Her prophecy [to Pushkin] was . . . that *he would live long if in the thirty-seventh year of his life he could avoid some disaster* brought to him either by a white horse, by blond hair, or by a white man (weisser Ross, weisser Kopf, weisser Mensch) [emphasis added]."

Kirchhof's prophecy of forthcoming disaster in Pushkin's life, as we have already seen, had kept him on edge since age nineteen. In 1833, Pushkin discussed a natural disaster (the Neva flood) that drives its hero insane in *The Bronze Horseman*. In 1835, the hero of "A Pilgrim" exclaims about the time of the disaster: "It's coming! it's close, close the time . . ." Logically, the year 1834 should not have been any exception: Pushkin is waiting for disaster and fears it. Why? We must not forget that Kirchhof had told Pushkin about his death "in the thirty-seventh year of his life." And this time was getting close indeed.

Magnifying Glass 2

What else makes Kirchhof similar to the queen of spades? A visual resemblance as well. On classic Russian cards, the queen of spades wears a black dress and black shawl. P. Karatygin wrote about Kirchhof: "*A black woollen dress and a similar shawl* with a narrow Turkish hem were her permanent attire [emphasis added]."

Although the similarity between the card and a Russianized German fortune-teller cannot be proved by anything but the fact of a "grasping" poetic eye, Pushkin's ability to connect different things still seems to be a weighty reason to suppose that he perceived it so.

Still, why does the queen of spades "kill" the ace: "bad" Kirchhof—an "important man"? In order to answer to this question we need to return to the three and the seven, that is, to make a U-turn.

U-TURN: THREE, SEVEN

We remember that Pushkin indeed believed in Kirchhof's words that his death would come "either from a white horse, or blond hair, or a white man." We remember that he tried to abuse almost everybody who fit this description.

Magnifying Glass 3

Sobolevsky wrote: "Pushkin is very superstitious, and that is why when chance brings him together with a man who has all these features he starts to think: is not precisely he that homme-fatal? *He even tries to irritate him in order to tempt his fate as soon as possible* [emphasis added]."

We also remember that Pushkin told many people that his death would occur "because of his wife." I have already mentioned that all "documented" fixations on Kirchhof's prophecy end with Pushkin's marriage. Taking into consideration the fact that Pushkin was very superstitious; that he supposed his wife to be "dangerous"; and that d'Antès, his future murderer, was exactly a "blond" man might make us think that Pushkin was not sufficiently alert for the first time in his life. For all this, however, I have a different explanation.

"D'Antès," writes Prince Viazemsky, "arrived in Petersburg in 1833 and attracted Pushkin's contemptuous attention."[57] Thus, it is not true that Pushkin was not alert. D'Antès did attract Pushkin's attention, though nothing had yet started between d'Antès and Pushkin's wife. At the same time, Pushkin did not try to "irritate him." Why not? In 1833, and for the first time, Pushkin writes about the coming disaster. Does he feel its probability from such a person as d'Antès? I doubt it, but Pushkin is alert. We should not forget that he was constantly asking himself, "is not precisely he that homme-fatal?" Or, if we translate it into the terms of *The Queen of Spades*, that "important man, *tuz*, the ace."

Moreover, Pushkin is a gambler, and faro, as we learned, is a meta-

Two Superstitious Men

physical game; that is, it is a representation of gambling with one's own destiny. From Kirchhof he had learned that the thirty-seventh year of his life would be the most dangerous. And here the personal code of *The Queen of Spades* starts. Let us recall the story. The following passage describes the first day of Hermann's gambling:

> Hermann took a bank note out of his pocket and gave it to Chekalinskii, who after a quick glance at it placed it on Hermann's card.
> Chekalinskii proceeded to deal. A nine fell to his right, and a three to his left.
> "It's a winner," said Hermann, showing his card.

The second day is described thus:

> The next evening he was at Chekalinskii's again. The host was dealing. The punters made room for Hermann as soon as he approached the table. Chekalinskii bowed to him affably.
> Hermann waited until a new deal began; then he led a card, placing both his original forty-seven thousand and his win of the previous night on it.
> Chekalinskii began dealing. A jack fell to his right and a seven to his left.
> Hermann turned his seven face up.
> Everybody gasped. . . . [58]

The banker Chekalinskii is, of course, that person whom Iurii Lotman called "a dummy in the hands of the Unknown Factors behind his back." If it is Pushkin who is playing over the head of his own Hermann, he now faces his destiny foretold by the German fortune-teller. Between the two victories—of the three and the seven—the action of the story moves so fast as to recall a film script more than "conventional" prose narrative. It is as if Pushkin wanted to slip through it as soon as possible; to win—on the three and seven—as soon as possible. Thirty-seventh year. Three and seven win. Pushkin wins his fatal years back. Gambling with his own fate. Winning both numbers from death. Exorcising on paper.

RETURN: THE QUEEN OF SPADES, ACE

However, the exorcism is not over yet. The "important man" whom Pushkin fears must be—metaphysically—eliminated as well. And here the queen of spades comes up. But before we start disclosing why exactly she, "Kirchhof," was chosen for this role, it is important to note that Pushkin had displayed a fight between an ace and a queen even before *The Queen of Spades*.

In 1825, he wrote some fragments now known as "Sketches for a Project about Faust" ("Nabroski k zamyslu o Fauste"). In it, Pushkin planned to describe a journey of Faust and Mephistopheles to Hell. Interestingly enough, two of these nine fragments are devoted to describing a card game. What is more, it is quite unclear who the players are because both fragments are written in the form of an impersonal dialogue. Or, to be more exact, only one part is known for sure, and that is Death herself. Here is the first fragment:

>—Что козырь?—Черви.—Мне ходить.
>—Я бью.—Нельзя ли погодить?
>—Беру.—Кругом нас обыграла.
>—Эй, смерть! Ты, право, сплутовала.
>—Молчи! ты глуп и молоденек.
>Уж не тебе меня ловить.
>Ведь мы играем не из денег,
>А только б вечность проводить!

>—What is trump?—Hearts.—Then, I start.
>—I cover.—Would you wait a minute, please.
>—I take.—You beat us completely.
>—Listen, death! You have really cheated.
>—Shut up! you are stupid and too young.
>It is not for you to catch me.
>We are not playing for money,
>but just to spend eternity.

Of course, we can guess the identity of the players. The one who asks to wait a minute is probably Faust. The other one, who accuses Death of cheating, is most likely Mephistopheles. Still, the dialogue is impersonal, that is, without names, and only Death is given a name and even a philosophical statement in the end.

The second fragment (and the ninth in the series) is even more impersonal:

>—Об этом думают двояко;
>Обычай требовал, однако,
>Соизволенья моего,
>Но, впрочем, это ничего.
>Вы знаете, всегда я другу
>Готова оказать услугу . . .
>Я дамой . . .—Крой!—Я бью тузом . . .
>—Позвольте, козырь.—Ну, пойдем . . .

Two Superstitious Men

>—About this, people think in two ways;
>custom demanded though
>my authorization,
>but it is fine by me.
>You know, I am always ready
>to do a service for a friend . . .
>I lead with a queen . . . —Cover!—I cover yours with an ace . . .
>—Excuse me, it's a trump.—Then I lead . . .

We can guess that the one who speaks the most here is again Death. Moreover, Death plays both the queen and the ace. What cards the other players are using is unclear, although it is said that when Death leads with a queen one of the players (Faust?) answers with a trump. Again, the suit of trump is very equivocal. In the first fragment it was mentioned that trump is hearts. However, the Russian word for "hearts," *chervi*, is ambiguous, because it also means "maggots." Because the game takes place in Hell, and the major player is Death, the sepulchral wordplay on "maggots-hearts" is more than appropriate. In response to Death's lead of the queen her vis-à-vis answers with maggots. Only a queen and an ace are named as cards in both fragments, and they are in the hands of Death.

Consequently, if we turn now to *The Queen of Spades*, Death—from whom Pushkin, over Hermann's head, has already won his thirty-seventh year back—still holds an ace and a queen, and either card can win. Why does the queen of spades beat an ace?

We remember from the epigraph that the queen of spades, "Kirchhof," means ill will. For Pushkin, the ace, his "important man" on whom his life hangs, means the same. The latter is, of course, more menacing. Why is this so? Let us recall Kirchhof's prophecy: Pushkin "would live long if in his thirty-seventh year . . ." Kirchhof still left him a chance! Pushkin, by eliminating the ace, is simultaneously eliminating this "if."

The queen of spades, who, after Hermann's loss on the ace, "screwed up her eyes and grinned," actually produces her physiognomic gestures for both Hermann and Pushkin. For Hermann she is the old countess, who, of course, celebrates her victory over the person who pushed her (to death!) to reveal the secret of the three cards. For Pushkin, she is the fortune-teller Kirchhof, who is screwing up her eyes as if saying: "What a really great son of a bitch you are, Pushkin! ("Ай да Пушкин, ай да сукин сын!") You did it! You will live long now!" And then she grins in approval. Moreover, the queen of spades, *pikovaia dama* or *dama pik* in Russian, provokes a linguistic development almost on the spot. In Dahl's famous dictionary, which reflects the usage of Pushkin's time, *pikovaia dama* is followed in one article by the words *pik* (a peak) and *pikirovat'sia* (to compete, to make an effort to outdo somebody).⁵⁹ Is it not possible to suppose that those meanings were also included in Pushkin's choice of exactly *pikovaia dama* as the suit to surpass the ace, that is, his predicted ill fate? We probably would not be stretching a point if we supposed that Pushkin, with his linguistic gift, had also taken these meanings into consideration: with the queen of spades he had competed with fate, outdone the ace, and mounted the peak of victory.

There is enough in the story to indicate that its numbers, otherwise nonsensical, are meaningful only for Pushkin and nobody else. He is, so to speak, fencing at cards with Death. On paper, he exorcised the powerful prophecy which, nevertheless, came true in 1837, a bit more than two years after *The Queen of Spades* had attempted to overcome it.

LAST DIGRESSION: WHY D'ANTÈS?

> When once Alexander had given way to fears
> of supernatural influence, his mind grew so
> disturbed and so easily alarmed that, if the
> least unusual or extraordinary thing happened,
> he thought it a prodigy or a presage . . . So
> miserable a thing is incredulity and contempt
> of divine power on the one hand, and so miserable, also, superstition on the other, which like
> water, where the level has been lowered,
> flowing in and never stopping, fills the mind
> with slavish fears and follies, as now in
> Alexander's case.
> —Plutarch, *Alexander* ⁶⁰

The mystery surrounding the last year of Pushkin's life remains puzzling. Why exactly did the poet choose d'Antès as the target of his general irritation? On this matter, many of Pushkin's contemporaries were somehow in solidarity. N. Ivanitsky commented:

In the last year of his life, Pushkin was decidedly looking for death. There was some kind of a psychological riddle. Nobody could have known the reason, because Pushkin was surrounded by spies: his every word, spoken in the study to the sincerest of his friends, was known to the government. Thus, what was in his heart is known only to God . . . Of course, Pushkin's wife was charged, that she had an affair with d'Antès. But Sologub says this is an absolute nonsense. Pushkin's wife was a beauty, and her worshippers were legion. It is no wonder that d'Antès also worshipped her as a beautiful woman;

but there were no liaisons between those two. People suspect another reason. Pushkin's wife was a maid of honor, that is why people think that she had had liaisons with the tsar. From this, it is clear why Pushkin was looking for death and throwing himself on anybody and everybody. There was nothing left for his soul but death [emphasis added].[61]

A "psychological riddle," as Ivanitsky put it, or the real reason for the duel, was indeed a fascinating question for high society. However, the general explanation was unanimous: Pushkin had been gambling with his own life, playing with Death (like his own Faust). "Khomiakov," noted another contemporary, "truly believes that Pushkin had become tired of life and that he used the first pretext to lose it, because the anonymous libel [that Pushkin was a cuckold] was not insulting enough to make a duel inevitable."[62] Khomiakov's own assessment seems to be even shrewder. He asserted:

Cheap rehearsal of Onegin and Lensky, cheap and overly early end. No factual reason for a duel existed, and Pushkin's challenge shows that his poor heart had been exhausted long ago and that *he wanted to risk his life in order either to get rid of it at once or to resume it* [emphasis added]."[63]

The italicized statement is sharp. Indeed, Pushkin's choice, if we adjust it with Kirchhof's prophecy together with *The Queen of Spades,* must have been exactly as Khomiakov put it: either to die in a duel with a "blond man" (in the thirty-seventh year of his life) or to continue living (to win on the three and the seven, killing the ace). A superstitious man, Pushkin was most probably sure that he would win, since he had already exorcised his bad luck in the story. That is why he, the desperate gambler, went into battle: to *verify* whether he was right or not. He truly believed in what had been coded.

II

"Our modern culture, genuine and original, our modern mentality and spiritual existence started with Pushkin. Pushkin erected the house of our spiritual life, the building of Russian historical consciousness. Lermontov was its first tenant," wrote Boris Pasternak.[64] I am not going to analyze all the possible meanings of this statement. Lermontov as Pushkin's "successor" in Russian culture is a huge topic. One side of this "succession" seems to me unusually fascinating, however: that in the building of Pushkin's superstitions, to use Pasternak's metaphor, Lermontov was quite at home.

Lermontov's entire literary career was connected with Pushkin's name, and its actual start, at least the beginning of Lermontov's fame, coincides with the poem "The Death of a Poet," written after Pushkin's fatal duel. Here, Lermontov famously blamed the powers that be for Pushkin's demise, in the spirit of a political lampoon, hinting at the tsar himself. I do not wish to discuss the overall quality of this poem; the important thing for me about it is that Lermontov was *verifying* himself on Pushkin, showing everybody who should be Pushkin's successor, who should take the baton. Using Pasternak's words again, Lermontov was attempting to move as fast as possible into the house of Pushkin.

However, in Lermontov's case, as in any genuine one, succession does not mean parroting. Quite the opposite, it rather means repulsion: the desire to demonstrate that he as an author is *different*. In relation to Pushkin, Lermontov did not leave any statement comparable to his famous poetic one about Byron ("No, I am not Byron, I am different..."), but his mental "duel" with Pushkin's fame, the struggle for his own "difference," occurred, I believe, on a *coded* level. One of those coded battles, which can be called an exorcism of Pushkin's presence in his own work, we will observe in Lermontov's treatment of the issue of a superstitious man. And for the field of this battle, Lermontov chose precisely *The Queen of Spades*.

LERMONTOV'S APPROACH TO PUSHKIN 1: DOES DIFFERENT MEAN SIMILAR?

"A stake," says a Russian proverb, "can be knocked out only with another stake." Although a bit aggressively, this proverb implies that like can be treated only by like. In the case of literature and specifically of Lermontov versus Pushkin, this would mean genres, or more exactly, prose attacked in and by other prose. The most vivid piece of Lermontov's prose, dedicated entirely to the topic of superstitions, is the last story of his novel *A Hero of Our Time:* "The Fatalist."

Let us recall its plot. Pechorin, the hero of the seven pieces of the novel, finds himself at a Cossack settlement. There, the officers mostly spend their time playing cards. One of them is Lieutenant Vulich, whose only passion is gambling. One day they begin to argue about whether predestination exists. Vulich set out to prove that it does, that everybody dies at his or her allotted time. Pechorin offers him a wager. Vulich picks up a pistol and offers to play Russian roulette. Pechorin prognosticates his death that very night. The officers, however, are against such an experiment and beg Vulich not to try it. Instead, Vulich asks Pechorin to take a card from the table and throw it upward. As it comes down, Vulich pulls the trigger but the pistol misfires. The officers think it was not loaded, but Vulich shoots once again and brings down somebody's cap that was hanging in the room. After this, Pechorin says that he has begun to believe in predestination. In the early morning, however, Pechorin discovers that Vulich was indeed killed that very night by a drunk Cossack. The latter has now locked himself in an empty hut and refuses to submit. Pechorin decides to test his own destiny and goes after the Cossack, who shoots at him but barely misses. The Cossack is captured.

At first glance, Lermontov's story has nothing in common with Pushkin's *The Queen of Spades*, at least on the level of the plot. The few things that unite them are the card game, Vulich's and Hermann's passion for gambling, and their metaphysical substrate (three unearthly cards and the issue of secret fate). However, the beginning of "The Fatalist" already hints at Pushkin's work. The story, narrated in the first person by Pechorin himself, begins:

> I once happened to spend two weeks at a Cossack settlement on our left flank. An infantry battalion was also stationed there and officers used to assemble at each other's quarters in turn, and play cards in the evening. On one occasion, having tired of boston and thrown the cards under the table, we sat on for a very long time at Major S——'s place.[65]

And here is how *The Queen of Spades* begins:

> There was a card party at the house of Narumov, an officer of the Horse Guards. The long winter night passed imperceptibly; it was close to five in the morning when the company sat down to supper. Those who had won were eating with good appetite; the others sat lost in thought before their empty plates. But champagne was brought in, and the conversation grew lively, with everyone joining in.[66]

Both stories continue with "conversations" after the introductory paragraph: about three magic cards in *The Queen of Spades* and about "the Moslem belief in a man's fate being written in heaven" in "The Fatalist." In addition, Lermontov sustains Pushkin's principle: his story is *not* about a real card game, but about gambling with destiny. As in Pushkin's story, the major gambler is a foreigner: Vulich "was of Serbian origin, as was apparent from his name," indicates Lermontov. Why did he decide to make him a nonnative, too? Vulich's portrait might answer this question:

> Lieutenant Vulich's looks corresponded perfectly to his nature. A tall stature, a swarthy complexion, black hair, black piercing eyes . . .—all this seemed to blend in such a way as to endow him with the air of a *special being, incapable of sharing thoughts and passions with those whom fate had given him for companions* [emphasis added].[67]

Vulich is a foreigner because he is *different* from others. The declaration of difference, besides being a key point of Romanticism in general, nevertheless takes on an additional meaning in the case of Vulich, because Pechorin, Lermontov's alter ego, is different, too. Or, as Vissarion Belinsky registered it long ago, Vulich "is very much alike Pechorin. Himself, Pechorin is here an active participant, and even more in the foreground than the story's hero [Vulich]."[68] Vulich's difference is created by contrast with Pechorin's, which is not exotic but, so to speak, predestined.

Pushkin's Hermann is also different. Pushkin writes about him:

> Hermann was the son of a Russified German, who had left him a little capital. . . . Since *he was also reserved and proud, his comrades rarely had occasion to laugh at his excessive thriftiness. He had strong passions and a fiery imagination,* but his resoluteness saved him from the usual lapses of youth. *He was, for example, a gambler at heart but never touched a card.* . . . *Yet at the same time he would sit by the card table whole nights and follow with feverish trembling the different turns of the game* [emphasis added].[69]

Hermann's portrait closely matches Vulich's, about whom Lermontov writes that "there was only one passion of which he made no secret—the gaming passion." Pushkin, as I have attempted to demonstrate, was playing with his own destiny over the head of his hero, leaving the hero defeated and insane. Lermontov, in the name of Pechorin, also gambles with destiny, when the latter subdues the drunken Cossack.[70] What is more, Vulich, Pechorin's contrast, also wins in the beginning (like Hermann), but finally loses (his life), while Pechorin is victorious. If we try to create pairs for both stories, they will look as follows: Pechorin (read, Lermontov) wins when gambling; Pushkin wins, too. Vulich first wins, but then loses; Hermann—the same. Does this mean then that *The Queen of Spades* is mirrored in "The Fatalist"? In order to answer this question, let us turn to the actual cards employed in Lermontov's story.

LERMONTOV'S APPROACH TO PUSHKIN 2: TWO CARDS

Not one but two situations in "The Fatalist" are directly connected with cards. One we have already noted: Pechorin throws a card upward. Vulich shoots and wins. We will return to this situation a bit later. However, the first moment connected to cards occurs before that, and it is also related to Vulich's reputation as a fearless gambler, or, in other words, a fatalist.

Two Superstitious Men

It was rumored that, one night, while on active duty, he dealt out the cards at stuss [a kind of faro] on his pillow; he was having formidable luck. All of a sudden, shots were heard, the alarm was sounded, there was a general scamper for weapons. "Set your stake for the whole bank," cried Vulich, without rising, to one of the keenest punters. "All right, I set it upon a seven," answered the other, as he rushed off. Despite the general confusion, Vulich went on dealing all alone, and the seven came up for the punter.

When he reached the front line, the firing there was already intense. Vulich paid no attention either to the bullets or the swords of the Chechens: he was in search of his fortunate punter. "The seven turned up on your side," he shouted on seeing him at last in the firing line . . . , and, on coming closer, took out his purse and his wallet and handed them to the lucky gamester, despite the latter's protest that this was not an appropriate place for payment.[71]

This episode, purely decorative in itself, is arresting because of a detail that is almost impossible to overlook (especially since Lermontov points it out twice): the rank of the card—a *seven*. Vulich's partner, a punter, stakes on the seven and wins; Vulich, the banker, loses. Thus, the story begins not with Vulich's win but with his loss. But why did Lermontov care about the *exact* rank of the card on which Vulich loses? Or do we only imagine that he did, because it happens to be a match with Pushkin's? In order to clear the entire picture up, let us return to the situation in which Vulich does win: when he shoots at a card.

"Mr. Pechorin," he [Vulich] added, "take a card and throw it up into the air."
I took from the table what I vividly remember turned out to be the ace of hearts and threw it upwards. Everyone held his breath; all eyes, expressing fear and a kind of vague curiosity, switched back and forth from the pistol to the fateful ace which quivered in the air and slowly came down. The moment it touched the table, Vulich pulled the trigger . . . the pistol misfired![72]

Here, Lermontov once again decisively underscores the card's rank ("I vividly remember . . .") and notes it twice, as had been the case with the seven: "the ace of hearts," "the fateful ace." Thus, the card on which Vulich wins is the *ace*. But why would the writer emphasize a similar detail (the card's rank) twice in the only two situations connected with cards in the entire story if it did not have great importance for him? He forces the reader to notice those names, wants us to remember both cards. Still, why?

We have seen that Lermontov already hints at Pushkin's *The Queen of Spades* in the very beginning of his story; moreover, his Vulich bears a physical resemblance to Hermann. Let us now compare the card circumstances in *The Queen of Spades* with those in "The Fatalist." In the first, Hermann wins on the three and the seven and loses on the ace. In the second, Vulich loses on the seven and wins on the ace. Does Lermontov want us to notice that the ranks of *two* cards are the *same* as in Pushkin, while their function in his story is the *opposite*? That the seven, which wins in Pushkin's story, loses in his? That the ace, which is defeated in Pushkin, becomes triumphant here? If this is so, then the important question to ask will be about the missing third card from *The Queen of Spades,* the three. Where is it? There are no other cards, or even numbers, mentioned in "The Fatalist." Probably, the shortest way to discover the missing three would be to appeal to the unusual composition of Lermontov's novel.

LERMONTOV'S APPROACH TO PUSHKIN 3: THE DUEL BEFORE THE MISSING CARD IS FOUND

Lermontov saved "The Fatalist" for the novel's finale, although it was actually the second of the novel's seven pieces to be published (in 1839, in the periodical *Otechestvennye zapiski* (*Notes of the Fatherland*). The first to appear there was "Bela," which later became the opening story in *A Hero of Our Time*. Thus, the two stories with which Lermontov went public before the others ultimately parenthesize all the events in the novel, taking place at different times. Why did Lermontov keep "The Fatalist" for the end?

On this matter, Boris Eichenbaum, probably one of the most perceptive readers of the novel, wrote:

> "The Fatalist" plays the role of a double-finale: it is not only the ending of "Pechorin's Journal" [the novel contains two other stories told by Pechorin in the first person: "Taman" and "Princess Mary"], it also locks up the entire "chain of stories," that makes the novel. The author saved himself from the traditional duty to tell us about the hero's further life and his death, because he had already told us about those earlier ("Maksim Maksimich" and "Introduction to Pechorin's Journal"). The problem of a finale is solved differently: in the foundation of the last story was put a question of "fate," of "predestination," of "fatalism"—the question that is characteristic for the *Weltanschauung* and the behavior of the people of the 1830s (for the post-Decembrist era). This finale was also prepared by events inside the novel, because in both "Taman" and "Princess Mary" the hero finds himself on the edge of death.[73]

In his last comment, Eichenbaum is especially observant: "Princess Mary," the story that precedes "The Fatalist," actually prepares the ground for it in many respects. In that story Pechorin survives the duel with another hero who is contrasted to him—Grushnitski. As Viktor Manuilov pointed out, "For Pechorin, Vulich is just an experimental tool: by offering him a wager, Pechorin very probably provokes Vulich to suicide. Pechorin puts himself to exactly the same experiment when facing the loaded pistol of Grushnitski."[74] In other words, in both stories Pechorin is a gambler who plays with his life, and no less so than Vulich or Grushnitski. If Pechorin is Lermontov's alter ego, then Lermontov is playing with his destiny over the heads of two other characters, too.

Indeed, the game that was started in "Princess Mary" continues in "The Fatalist." Although I fully agree with Eichenbaum's reasons for why "The Fatalist" was chosen to become the novel's finale, there is still a question that might be asked here. Yes, "The Fatalist" shares a major issue—gambling with life—with "Princess Mary." However, if this is so, why was it and not "Princess Mary" placed as the novel's ending? If the issue is the same in both, why not put "The Fatalist" before "Princess Mary," and thus end the novel with probably the best written of the all the seven parts? Would it be, as Eichenbaum claims, that doing so would not emphasize the philosophical views of Lermontov and his generation? Or, perhaps, there is some other glue that keeps these two stories in the order Lermontov gave them?

Let us turn to the Pechorin-Grushnitski duel in "Princess Mary." Grushnitski calls Pechorin out and, with the help of his second, they plan to deceive him—to load only Grushnitski's pistol. By accident, Pechorin eavesdrops on their conspiracy. Already on the dueling ground he comes up with a sudden idea to foil their plan:

> Well, this is what I have thought up. Do you see at the summit of that sheer cliff on the right, a narrow bit of flat ground? There is a drop of about three hundred feet or more from there; below, there are sharp rocks. Each of us will take his stand on the very edge of the shelf, and in this way even a light wound will be fatal.[75]

Does not Pechorin's idea sound like that of someone who has already taken part in "The Fatalist"? In fact, he has already done so, because the events described there precede those in "Princess Mary" chronologically, that is, in biographical, not novelistic time. Still, even if we do not know about this and only Pechorin does, in what way would the novel be different for the reader were the two stories to change places? In both stories, Pechorin is brave and fatalistic. What is more, his bravery in "Princess Mary" would be probably more "motivated" for the reader if the latter already knew the events in "The Fatalist" (one more reason to think the order of the stories should have been reversed).

Grushnitski agrees to Pechorin's idea. Both stand on the cliff, and Pechorin hopes that Grushnitski's conscience will be awakened and that he will discharge his pistol into the air; if not, the duel would become murder, because Grushnitski knows that Pechorin's pistol is not loaded. They draw lots, and Grushnitski is to shoot first. If we translate this situation into faro, Pechorin will be the punter (he takes the risk), while Grushnitski is the banker (he has the situation in his hands). Pechorin describes this situation later:

> I decided to give Grushnitski every advantage; I wished to test him. A spark of magnanimity might awaken in his soul—and then everything would turn out for the best; but vanity and weakness of character were to triumph! . . . *I wished to give myself the full right to show him no quarter, if fate spared me.* Who has not concluded similar agreements with his conscience? [emphasis added][76]

The argument of fate is precisely that of a card player, of Vulich's student from "The Fatalist."

To Pechorin's bitterness, he notices that Grushnitski aims not into the air but straight at his forehead—a sign that he wants to kill in cold blood. At the last moment Grushnitski hesitates but nevertheless shoots. The bullet grazes Pechorin's knee, but he manages not to fall off the cliff. When his turn comes, Pechorin announces that his pistol is not loaded. Despite the indignation of Grushnitski's second, he demands that it be loaded, and Pechorin kills his opponent.

If we follow the plot of the duel we find nothing that might help us to discover the "missing card." However, if we pay attention to what Lermontov underscores by means of word repetition, we may be more successful. Let us make a U-turn to the very beginning of the duel.

U-TURN: THE MISSING CARD, OR WHETHER PECHORIN BELIEVED IN OMENS

Pechorin and his second, Dr. Werner, approach the dueling ground. Pechorin's narrative runs as follows:

> Within me there are two persons: one of them lives in the full sense of the word, the other cogitates and judges him. The first will, perhaps, in an hour's time, take leave of you and the world forever, while the other . . . what about the other? . . . Look, doctor, do you see on that cliff on the right *three* black figures? Those are our adversaries, I believe."
>
> We set off at a trot.

Two Superstitious Men

> In the bushes at the foot of the cliff, *three* horses were tied. We tied our horses there too, and clambered up a narrow path to a flat ledge, where Grushnitski was awaiting us with the Captain of Dragoons and his other second. . . .[77]

This episode contains exactly the same device as in "The Fatalist," in which numbers/cards were pointed out twice. There, they were the seven and ace; here, it is the number three. This number, and that is especially important, belongs to Pechorin's enemies, who are ignobly planning to murder him, as both we and he know. Moreover, Pechorin's thoughts, just before the number was emphasized, are about death, his probable defeat in the duel. Why did Lermontov specify the number if it did not have special meaning for Pechorin, who, before the number was named, doubted the outcome of the duel? After the number is named, however, Pechorin no longer thinks about death and actually promises Grushnitski that he will kill him.

> "It seems to me," he [Werner] said, "that both parties having shown their readiness to fight, and having thus satisfied their readiness to fight, and having thus satisfied the demands of honor, you might, gentlemen, talk matters over and close the affair amicably."
>
> "I'm willing," I said.
>
> The captain gave Grushnitski a wink, and *he, thinking that I was scared, assumed a proud air, although up to then a dull pallor had been spread over his cheeks* [emphasis added].[78]

Before we continue, let us take a short break here to recall the state of Vulich in the ace situation. Pechorin describes it:

> I looked fixedly into his eyes, but he countered my probing glance with a calm and steady gaze, and *his pale lips smiled; but despite his coolness, I seemed to decipher the imprint of death upon his pale face* [emphasis added].[79]

Both of Pechorin's opponents are described similarly before the beginning of the mortal combat. Moreover, in the continuation of the Pechorin-Grushnitski dialogue, after Werner has tried to make peace between them, Pechorin's thought, or more exactly his confidence in Grushnitski's death, is remarkably similar to his thoughts in "The Fatalist" in relation to Vulich's death.

> "Explain your terms," he [Grushnitski] said, "and whatever I can do for you, you may be assured . . ."
>
> "Here are my terms: this very day you will publicly retract your slander and will apologize to me."

Writing as Exorcism

"Sir, I am amazed that you dare offer such things to me!"
"What else could I offer you?"
"We shall fight."
I shrugged my shoulders.
"As you please; but consider—one of us will certainly be killed."
"My wish is that it may be you."
"And I'm convinced of the opposite."
He lost countenance, colored, then burst into forced laughter [emphasis added].[80]

It is an interesting psychological document, this dialogue. Pechorin, who takes a huge risk here because his pistol is not loaded, nevertheless behaves like one who is absolutely sure that he will triumph. Yet, just a few moments earlier, he had been filled with gloomy speculations regarding the outcome of the duel. On the contrary, Grushnitski, who should be confident because his pistol is loaded and thus his position is risk free, nevertheless shows a hesitancy one would not expect. But why is Pechorin so sure that Grushnitski will die? Because for him the three is, so to speak, his opponent's unlucky card or, more exactly, he knows that it will be unlucky. How can he? Because he had read *The Queen of Spades*.

Since the events of "The Fatalist" had already taken place before the duel in "Princess Mary," Pechorin knows that Vulich, his former opponent, had lost on the seven and won on the ace. That is why he "knows" that the three (number three) has to be unlucky for his new opponent Grushnitski, and that is why "The Fatalist" was kept by Lermontov for the ending of his novel. Because "The Fatalist" was written before "Princess Mary," it was obviously too late to change the story's "numbers." In order to do that Lermontov would have needed to add an extra card situation connected with Vulich, and that would have been too transparent and thus tasteless; instead, he creates another duel in "Princess Mary," displays in it the number three, and thus maintains Pushkin's order of three, seven and ace, though he makes it less observable for the reader. Thus is Lermontov's private battle with Pushkin's text encoded here.

There is still one more way in which Lermontov's story intersects with Pushkin's.

The two future participants of the duel and their seconds climb up the cliff:

Suddenly, small stones noisily rolled down to our feet. What was it? *Grushnitski had stumbled.* The branch which he had grasped broke and he would have slid down on his back, had not his seconds supported him.

"*Take care!*" *I cried to him.* "*Don't fall beforehand: it's a bad omen. Remember Julius Caesar!*" [emphasis added][81]

Two Superstitious Men

Lermontov's creation of a bad omen for Grushnitski, as well as the fact that Pechorin notices it, is an open foreshadowing of the future events. Vladimir Nabokov writes in the comments to his translation that Pechorin's remark is "an allusion to the various bad omens that preceded Caesar's assassination as related in Plutarch's *Parallel Lives*."[82] This is certainly true. Moreover, to stumble was always one of the worst bad omens. Already Cicero had called it "the omen, from which weak minds tremble."[83] Pechorin, who has doubtless read both (Plutarch was a must-read in those days, and Cicero was a favorite author among the Decembrists), knows that Grushnitski has a "weak mind" and plays the superstitious card, because Grushnitski also knows what "to stumble" means. After all, even without Caesar the Russian folk superstition would be the same. According to it, "if the right foot stumbles—it is good luck, if the left—it is a disaster."[84] Pechorin, as we know, is almost always wide awake, and we can assume that Grushnitski stumbled with his left foot: when climbing up a hill, right-handed people usually grasp objects to support their climb (here, branches) with their left hand while their right foot does the stepping up; if Grushnitski had already made this step up when the branch broke in his left hand, then the foot he stumbled with had to be his left. In any case, Pechorin simultaneously mocks Grushnitski and believes that the mention of a bad omen will help his case. He also believes, because he is a fatalist: the ace had already won in "The Fatalist," and there is no way Grushnitski can do the same on the three. The reversed composition of the two stories helps underscore Pechorin's belief in predestination. That Pechorin shares this belief with his creator—the principal *difference* between Lermontov and Pushkin—we will see shortly.

FINAL APPROACH TO PUSHKIN: CAN ONE WIN WHEN PLAYING WITH HIS OR HER OWN DESTINY?

In 1840, after a bloody battle with Circassian tribesmen on the river Valerik, Lermontov wrote to his friend A. Lopukhin: "I have begun to enjoy the war, and I am sure that for one who has gotten used to the strong sensations provided by this bank, there remain few pleasures that would not seem sickly sweet."[85] It is interesting that Lermontov uses the card term "bank" here: war as a card game. Of the entire statement Manuilov aptly comments: "these words would have been appropriate in Pechorin's journal."[86] After this same battle, Lermontov also composed a long poem, "Valerik," in which he confessed:

> Мой крест несу я без роптанья:
> То иль другое наказанье?
> Не все ль одно. Я жизнь постиг;

Судьбе, как турок иль татарин,
За все равно я благодарен;
У бога счастья не прошу
И молча зло переношу.
Быть может, небеса востока
Меня с ученьем их пророка
Невольно сблизили. . . .[87]

I bear my cross without grumbling:
this or that punishment?
Does it matter? I have realized this life;
to fate, like a Turk or a Tatar,
I am equally grateful for everything;
I don't ask God for happiness
and silently endure evil.
Probably, the Moslem heaven
unwillingly drew me close
to its prophet. . . .

Do these lines of Lermontov echo the subject of the conversation with which "The Fatalist" starts? "We discussed," Pechorin, the soon-to-become fatalist writes, "the fact that the Moslem belief in a man's fate being written in heaven finds also among us Christians many adherents; each related various unusual occurrences in proof or refutation."[88]

As much as Lermontov is Pechorin, the characters in the novel who are contrasted to Pechorin—that is, Grushnitski and Vulich—are actually one personage, too. This personage, as Manuilov called him, is the "tool" of Pechorin's experiments on his own life. This "collective" character, though he does win on the ace and correspondingly loses on the three and the seven, is nevertheless doomed by fate. But, just to recall the rhetorical question of the poem, "Does it matter?"

The Queen of Spades is mirrored in Lermontov's stories, and the card situations in both are mirrorlike: what in Pushkin is, so to speak, right, becomes left in Lermontov; if in Pushkin particular cards win, they lose in Lermontov, and vice versa. Still, this difference would be just a fact of the obstinacy of acting against Pushkin, if Lermontov's "Does it matter?" had not existed. In so doing—that is, by changing the function of Pushkin's cards in his prose—Lermontov insists on the difference between his *Weltanschauung* and Pushkin's.

Pushkin believed that if omens are read the right way one can avoid predestination and thus that fate can be changed. This kind of exorcism—of the bad part of Kirchhof's prophecy, the struggle for the "if" in it—Pushkin performed in *The Queen of Spades* when creating his otherwise meaningless numerology. In order to assure himself that his exorcism was successful Pushkin tested his fate for real in the "bad" thirty-seventh year of his life.

Lermontov, who sees himself as Pushkin's successor, also gambles with fate but differently. He, wrote Viskovaty, "took special pleasure in testing his fate; danger or the probability of death made him witty, talkative, and gay."[89] And here is the difference. Lermontov tests his fate, but, unlike Pushkin, he does not struggle with it. In Lermontov's case, a superstitious man is a reckless one.

A FINAL DIGRESSION: LERMONTOV'S DUEL WITH MARTYNOV, OR WHY HE DID NOT SHOOT

The fatalistic behavior of Lermontov during the war was repeated in his fatal duel with Martynov. The contemporary writer Viktor Sosnora interestingly compares both:

> At the age of twenty, Lermontov is a cornet of the Life-Guards hussar regiment.... The young man writes to Lopukhina: if war comes, I will always be at the head. He was.... In the battle on the river Valerik Lermontov acts in the ground support column, he is an aide-de-camp, in that battle the losses are 2% among the officers, among the aides-de-camp—20%.... In the battle of October 10, Rufin Dorokhov [a prototype of Tolstoy's Dolokhov in *War and Peace*], a commander of the hundred selected cavalry fighters,... is wounded. Dorokhov passes the command to Lermontov. From then on the vanguard was called Lermontov's. N. A. Sultanov, who served in it, writes: "Anybody could become a member; one's head would have been shaven, he would have been ordered to grow a beard and given a double-barrelled gun with a bayonet. The cavalrymen were notable for their desperate bravery, their devotion to their commander, and their contempt of fire-arms.".... K. Kh. Mamaev writes: "Even during this march he [Lermontov] did not obey any procedure, and his vanguard, like a comet, wandered everywhere, appearing where it wished to be; in battle they looked for the most dangerous places.... In June, Charlotta [the tsarina] gives *A Hero of Our Time* to Nicholas [the tsar], Charlotta is ecstatic. Nicholas abruptly responds to it and again exiles Lermontov to the Caucasus, where he had already spent more than a year. On July 14, 1840 Nicholas writes to Charlotta: 'Happy journey, Mr. Lermontov, let him cleanse his head. Under bullets.' After eleven months and one day Lermontov was killed by a shot right through his chest.... People write that the seconds were hoping for a peaceful solution; but whom were they taking for the duelists?—that's the question, and here is the an-

Writing as Exorcism

swer: they were taking both for Lermontov. Let us recall Lermontov's code of honor: bayonet fight and swords, on the banner of his vanguard was written *contempt of fire-arms;* his duel with Martynov was his sixth, and he had never asked for quarter but at the same time had never taken a shot, not even once. This was known to Petersburg, Moscow, Nicholas, the seconds, Martynov also knew it. And despite having known it, he shot and killed. . . .[90]

Pushkin and Lermontov were both killed in a duel. Both were killed not by fate (or by superstition), but by their belief in it.

Chapter Three

Gogol's Nausea and Nossea

> ... 4. The highest sneezing speed on record registered at 103.6 miles per hour. 5. The sense of smell is directly connected to the limbic system in the brain, which is concerned with behavior, memory and emotion. ...
> —"Nine New Things to Know about Your Nose"

NIKOLAI GOGOL WAS an oddball, an eccentric, a strange man, in both his life and his literary art. The strangeness of his literary work—its novelty of language, its pre-Surrealist Surrealism—has been discussed and recorded by many critics, who exercised their wit in explicating it. In addition, some insightful investigations, especially those of Vikenty Veresaev in Russia and of Vladimir Nabokov and Simon Karlinsky in the United States, have focused on Gogol's human oddity, including his hidden sexuality.

One of the strangest and most intimate relationships Gogol maintained, however, was with his own self or, to be more precise, with his own long, almost Bergeracian nose. This synecdochal part of Gogol's own "I" was a magnet of his permanent cares and irritations. His Catullus-like, love-hate attitude toward his nose probably started in school, where Gogol was famous for being able to touch it with his lower lip—a neat party trick. Later in life, he simultaneously was afraid of injuring it by frostbite while traveling and lived in an apartment in Rome where the low temperature, as registered by Gogol's temporary roommate there, the Russian poet Nikolai Iazykov, always kept his nose blue.

His literary debut of 1829, a long Romantic narrative poem, failed because of its poetic clumsiness. The book, the remaining copies of which were bought back by its author and destroyed, was titled "Ganz Küchelgarten," a sign of Gogol's admiration for Wilhelm Küchelbecker. The latter, a Russian poet of German origin, was famous not only for his heavy eighteenth-century-like literary style, which Gogol faithfully imitated in his long poem, but also for his heavy, long nose, a feature constantly stressed by Pushkin in his friendly drawings of Küchelbecker.

Gogol did not dare to put his own name on the poem's cover but instead used the pseudonym V. Alov. In English, "alyi" means "royal red," and I believe that the color of his nose played a role in his choice of pseudonym. Also, if V. Alov is read as one word ("valov"), it suggests such verbs as *valit'sia* and *otvalivat'sia* ("to fall off" in English), which might well be connected with Gogol's anxiety of having his nose badly wounded by the weather.

Though Gogol's first pseudonymic connection with noses cannot be proved by anything more substantial than linguistic intuition, there is no question that they are significant in a number of subsequent works. Among these "nasal" works of Gogol the most famous is, of course, "The Nose" (1836). In "Nevsky Prospect" and *Dead Souls* noses can be nominated for the best supporting roles. Overall, then, one can say without a doubt that a nose is one of Gogol's psychological dominants.

DIGRESSION 1: NOSES STAR

In world literature, starring noses are not unusual. Two non-Gogolian examples come to my mind first (in addition to *Tristram Shandy*, which has frequently been cited in this regard): the long and sharp nose from *The Adventures of Pinocchio* by Carlo Collodi (1826–90), written from 1881 to 1883, and the huge one from *Cyrano de Bergerac* by Edmond Rostand (1868–1918), written in 1898. Is Gogol unique? Probably, the question should be put another way: do these two noses also play the role of plot engine as is the case in Gogol?

As for Pinocchio, the fact that this wooden puppet with a long nose comes to life as in some *Frankenstein* for children seems to be literarily more significant than the whole business of the long nose. Pinocchio's nose makes this marionette recognizable, but it does not make any serious difference to *Pinocchio*'s plot. Cyrano's nose as plot spring "shoots up" at the very beginning of Rostand's play, when he forces his enemy Valvert to insult it out loud (act 1, scene 4):[1]

> Valvert: Ah . . . your nose . . . hem! . . .
>   Your nose is . . . rather large!
> Cyrano *(gravely)*: Rather.
> Valvert *(simpering)*: Oh well—
> Cyrano *(cooly)*: Is that all?

Gogol's Nausea and Nossea

> Valvert *(turns away, with a shrug)*: Well, of course—
> Cyrano: Ah, no, young sir!
>> You are too simple. Why, you might have said—
>> Oh, a great many things! Mon dieu, why waste
>> Your opportunity? For example, thus:—
>> AGGRESIVE: I, sir, if that nose were mine,
>> I'd have it amputated—on the spot!
>> FRIENDLY: How do you drink with such a nose?
>> You ought to have a cup made specially.
>> DESCRIPTIVE: 'Tis a rock—a crag—a cape—
>> A cape? say rather, a peninsula!
>> INQUISITIVE: What is that receptacle—
>> A razor-case or a portfolio?
>> KINDLY: Ah, do you love the little birds
>> So much that when they come and sing to you,
>> You give them this to perch on? INSOLENT:
>> Sir, when you smoke, the neighbors must suppose
>> You chimney is on fire. CAUTIOUS: Take care—
>> A weight like that might make you topheavy. . . .
>> ELOQUENT: When it blows, the typhoon howls,
>> And the clouds darken. DRAMATIC: When it bleeds—
>> The Red Sea! ENTERPRISING: What a sign
>> For some perfumer! LYRIC: Hark—the horn
>> Of Rolland calls to summon Charlemagne! . . . [1]

Cyrano's nose as a metaphorical axis of the play's movement is even more striking than Cyrano's duel with Valvert, which follows this ironic monologue. The very fact that Cyrano's nose is huge drives the plot: Cyrano, a brave man and ingenious poet, cannot be loved by his adored, the beautiful Roxane. She chooses handsome but dull Christian instead, just because of the proportions of his nose. Still, Gogol's story about the nose is very special: he gives us *no reason* that the nose drives the plot; it happens neither because of the nose's size, nor because of any other distinguishing feature, except perhaps one—a small pimple on its top.

RETURN 1: APPROACHES TO THE PLOT

> Be patient, solemn nose,
> Serve in a world of prose
> The present moment well

Writing as Exorcism

> Nor surlily contrast
> Its brash ill-mannered smell
> With grand scents of the past. . . .
> —W. H. Auden, "Precious Five"

In 1836, Prince Petr Viazemsky writes in a letter: "Zhukovsky's Saturdays are flourishing . . . Only Gogol, whom Zhukovsky calls Gogolek [little Gogol], enlivens them with his stories. Last Saturday, he read us a story about a nose, which had suddenly disappeared from the face of some major. Hilarious!"[2] Indeed, the story's plot is built up around the strange event of a nose, which, or better who, escapes one morning from the face of Major Kovalev, when the latter was about to check a pimple on it; starts living socially as an "independent person" and a high official; but finally, miraculously, returns, or is returned, to his, now its, original place. In the meantime, Kovalev searches for his nose in various locales but nobody seems to notice he does not have one; Kovalev starts meeting his nose in various milieus, first as a human/nose bearing a high governmental rank who does not recognize him. Later, again a nose, it is suddenly brought back to Kovalev by a policeman, who says the nose had been caught in his/its attempt to cross the Russian border. When Kovalev asks the doctor to put a nose back in his face, the doctor refuses.[3]

How should we understand this bizarre plot? This problem remains open up till now and it has for a long time. Is it just an anecdote with no other meaning but playfulness, or does it have meaning that escapes our attention as did the nose from Kovalev's face? Both sides of this dilemma have their contributors. Thus, for instance, the advocates of "The Nose" as a nonsensical creation urge us to see the story either as sheer absurdity (Gary Saul Morson) or to accept it as "the most logic-defying piece of writing in Russian literature to this day" (Simon Karlinsky).[4] Both of these formulas for the nonsense make a great deal of sense. After all, the story's plot invokes questions that no satisfactory—that is, logical—answers fit, leaving what Morson aptly calls "the explanatory gap" in the story. He writes:

> Let us dwell for a moment on a few of the questions that a good explanation of this story's plot would have to answer: How does Kovalev lose his nose? If the barber cut it off when he shaved Kovalev on Wednesday, then why, as Kovalev asks, was the nose in its proper place on Thursday? Whether or not the barber cut it off, how did the nose get into the barber's roll? Why is there no scar; why is Kovalev's face "as flat as a pancake"? How does the nose grow to human size, and, still more perplexing, how does it become human? Given that it becomes biologically human, how does it become socially human? How does the nose develop a specific identity and a history—a rank

in the service and a set of acquaintances—and what happens to the memory of others to make them think they have known him? Does this perplexing event somehow manage to alter the past? How does the nose become a nose again, and, having done so, how does it resume its proper place on Kovalev's face?[5]

Since no logical answers can be given to these questions, both Morson and Karlinsky conclude that the entire plot of the story is meaningless, and absence of meaning in "The Nose" becomes its only true meaning. At the same time, the unanswerable questions Morson poses are all about "how" (how does the nose escape, and so on), while some of them could be asked with "why," too: Why does the nose escape, for example? The idea of precisely this way of questioning the story in order to reveal its concealed meaning belongs to the Russian poet and critic Innokenty Annensky. In his essay "The Problem of Gogolian Humor" Annensky writes:

Major Kovalev's nose got two weeks of originality. It happened because the Nose got offended, and he got offended because he had been offended, or, to be exact, could not bear any more his systematic offenses. [Among these "offenses" Annensky names the barber's way of shaving Kovalev while holding his nose with a bad-smelling hand, as well as Kovalev's granting permission to do so.] The hero of the story, i.e., its real hero, to my mind is the Nose. And the short story is the history of his two-weeks revenge.[6]

Annensky's essay, as is clear from its title, is about the comic in Gogol and is written in a corresponding style. His explication of the cause of the nose's departure, though truly brilliant for its insightful and almost Gogolian play, nevertheless fails to elucidate why it is Kovalev's *nose* that escapes, and not, for example, his leg, or an eye, or any other of the many important parts humans own. The only approach, which to this point has tried to reveal specifically this "why," is, unfortunately, Freudian. I say unfortunately, because it treats Gogol's oeuvre in a humorless way that nearly denies it its unsurpassed artistry, narrows everything to an identification of the nose as an encoded male sex organ, and sees in its escape a sign of Gogol's sexual destitution (Ivan Yermakov).[7]

Why a nose and not, roughly speaking, an eye, or, as Kovalev himself puts it, "a little toe"? I stress the word "why" superimposed on the "hows" in the questions Morson asked about Gogol's nonsensical story in order to get an answer with a positive "because": that is, that exactly a nose matters, and not "just because," which seems to be a logical and evasive half-answer in a case of "hows." The reason I think we might need to search for a positive answer is connected with Gogol's own awareness of his task as a writer, which he resolutely stated in his dramatic piece "Razviazka Revizora" ("The Finale of *The Inspector General*").⁸

When Gogol composed this essay in 1846 he intended to erase the generally accepted notion that his famous comedy was purely comic. When staged ten years before, *The Inspector General* had been an enormous success. Everybody loved it, from Tsar Nicholas I to those who were opposed to his type of regime. Despite his literary victory, however, Gogol was infuriated by the reception of the play and suddenly left Russia for Europe. For a decade, he was planning and hoping to change everybody's mind about what he had meant when writing this comedy.

Actually, its plot is as uncomplicated as that of many other "comedies of errors." Governmental officials in some small provincial town in nineteenth-century Russia are expecting an inspector general to arrive and thus to discover their many nasty abuses. They mistake a young man, Khlestakov, passing through their town back to St. Petersburg but stuck in it because of his empty pockets, for the feared inspector general. Khlestakov, at last, realizes they are mistaken and starts taking bribes from them. After Khlestakov leaves, the officials discover that he was not the inspector general, and the real one arrives.

What makes this comedy celebrated is not so much its plot as the way Gogol served it up, with various sides of the personages' linguistic characteristics unforgettably presented. Exactly this quality produces a comic effect bigger than would be predicted by a standard comedy of errors. So does the inventive "dumb scene" at its very end, when the astonishing news about the real inspector's arrival catches all the personages in the middle of their vivid discussion of Khlestakov's fraud and leaves them turned to stone and "sculptured" on stage as if by Medusa's gaze.

"The Finale of *The Inspector General*," however, stresses not the comedy's comic but also its allegorical essence. Gogol gives his readers/audience what he calls the true "key" to the comedy. According to this version, the provincial town of the play is not just an ordinary town but rather the "inner city" of our soul ("nash zhe dushevnyi gorod"); the nasty governmental officials stand for our human passions ("nashi strasti"); and the protagonist cheater Khlestakov is our false and mercenary social conscience ("vetrenaia svetskaia sovest', prodazhnaia, obmanchivaia sovest'"). Finally, the real inspector general is God, the judge of our human sins (as Gogol puts it: "frightful is that inspector general who awaits us at the grave's door"), and he is also our "awoken conscience" ("nasha prosnuvshaiasia sovest'").⁹

Reactions to this upgraded interpretation were ambivalent: some people (like the critic Sergei Aksakov) saw in it Gogol's autodistortion of his great comedy, while others (like the writer Stepan Shevyrev) found it almost too profound. Nevertheless, as the young Russian scholar Ilya Vinitsky properly puts it:

> Already the first evaluations of "The Finale of *The Inspector General*" gave two coordinates for further questions about this work: either Gogol slipped up and gave it in a "slick way of some justification post factum" (Mochul'skii) which distorts the original meaning of the comedy, or this is an auto-comment which comes organically from his entire writing and can be indeed a "key" to *The Inspector General*? . . . That point of view of the ideology in "The Finale of *The Inspector General*" as one which distorts the meaning of the famous comedy . . . does not find supporters at the present time. Scholars are right to see the organic nature of this auto-interpretation for the entire writer's work and link a concept of the "soul's city" and conscience's judgement with Gogol's earlier oeuvre.[10]

What seems substantial for Gogol in general, and via "The Finale . . ." in particular, is his desire to stress the comic-as-allegorical, to convey the gist of the latter by the means of the former; this points up Gogol's tendency to deliver his point in utterly enciphered forms. At least, "The Finale . . ." (or, rather, *The Inspector General* itself) is an excellent example of Gogol's work as a cipher clerk, and it is quite possible then that "The Nose," which is certainly a comic and nonsensical short story, might simultaneously be some sort of allegory as well.[11] Breathing through Gogolian noses in "Nevsky Prospect" and *Dead Souls* may help us in sniffing out their meaning.

DIGRESSION 2: THE NOSE PLANS ITS ESCAPE, BUT STAYS IN THE BATTLEFIELD OF ROMANTICISM

In "Nevsky Prospect," the story that precedes "The Nose" in the composition of the so-called Petersburg tales collected by Gogol together for the third volume of his *Writings* of 1842, one of its protagonists, Lieutenant Pirogov, nicknamed by Simon Karlinsky "a close cousin" of Major Kovalev because of his vulgarity, chases a young lady to her apartment, in which Gogol sets the following mise-en-scène:

> Before him [Pirogov] Schiller was sitting,—not the Schiller who wrote *Wilhelm Tell* and *The History of the Thirty-year War*, but the really famous Schiller, a tin-smith at Meshchanskaia [literally, Petty Bourgeois] Street. Nearby Schiller, Hoffmann was standing,—not Hoffmann-the-writer, but a fairly good shoemaker from Ofitserskaia [literally, Officers'] Street, a great buddy of Schiller's.

Schiller was drunk and was sitting on a chair, stamping his foot and narrating something heatedly. All this would not have amazed Pirogov, but he was amazed by an utterly strange dislocation of the bodies. Schiller was sitting, sticking out his rather thick nose and pointing his head up, while Hoffmann was holding him by this nose with two fingers and twirling the blade of his shoe-knife just below its surface. Both persons spoke German. . . ."I don't want, I don't need my nose!"—he [Schiller] was saying, swinging his hands.—"I am wasting on my one nose three tobacco pounds a month. . . . Twenty rubles and forty kopecks! I am a Swabian; I have a king in Germany. I don't want my nose! cut off my nose! here is my nose!" And if not for the sudden appearance of Lieutenant Pirogov, Hoffmann, without any doubt, would have cut off Schiller's nose for nothing, because he had already put his knife in a position as if he intended to cut out a sole.[12]

Schiller, as Pirogov finds out later, is the lady's husband. For our purposes, however, the nose, which is the focus of this mise-en-scène, is more substantial than the story's further development. The entire episode looks like a rehearsal of the events in "The Nose." Here, the potential escape of a nose is mentioned, only to be realized later, in the next story. In addition, Hoffmann's behavior, or rather his pose, almost doubles that of the barber in "The Nose," who, when shaving Kovalev, held his nose with a bad-smelling hand. Precisely the barber's manners, to recall Annensky, were the cause of the nose's disappearance: to the probability of being cut off, it preferred escape.

What is more, Gogol openly uses the names of Schiller and Hoffmann in order to double his comic effect. Two distinguished German authors hallowed by Romanticism are fighting for a nose. What is it, a parody of the Trojan war, with a nose as its Helen? Or a new version of *Sturm und Drang*, with a nose at its center? Heroic Schiller—and Gogol emphasizes specifically this part of Schiller's rich heritage by specifically mentioning his heroic drama *Wilhelm Tell* and his historiography—and mysterious Hoffman with his fantastic tales, are both acting here as drunks, that is, out of their minds. The story of "The Nose" is a remarkably grotesque combination of the work of Schiller and Hoffmann, a "history" in which the nose, its major "hero," makes a courageous escape from Kovalev's face in a Hoffmannesque way.

DIGRESSION 3: THE NOSE AS A CAUSE OF ROMANTIC LOSS

Besides being a history and a mystery, "The Nose" is a story about loss: Kovalev's loss of his nose. Heroic and mysterious Romanticism is also typically about loss; it is elegiac. Through its guru, Vasilii Zhukovsky, the father of the Russian elegy, this genre, in which the concept of loss is paramount, dominated Russia's Romantic stage. Konstantin Batiushkov (1787–1855); Alexander Pushkin (1799–1837); Evgeny Baratynsky (1800–44); Petr Viazemsky (1792–1878); Nikolai Iazykov (1803–47), who was later Gogol's roommate in Italy; and Mikhail Lermontov (1814–41) made elegy *the* genre, widely open to many imitators, both decent and bad. Gogol knew all of these poets except Batiushkov, who went insane in 1821, well before Gogol's literary debut. Sighs about lost love or joy became an obligatory part not just of poetry but also of social life. Here is a typical example of an average elegy by Dmitry Glebov (1789–1843), with its characteristic title "Memory of Love" ("Pamiat' liubvi"):

> В час сумрака, в сей час священный,
> Когда прохладу льет роса,
> Спешу на холм уединенный
> Смотреть ночные небеса.
> Мечтаю, что с высот эфирных
> Отшельники земной страны
> Слетают песни старины . . .
> И, волю дав воспоминанью,
> Я выражаю струн игрой,
> Как нежнй к чувств к очарованью
> Делился жизнию с тобой,
> И слышу: из воздушной бездны
> (Столь силен в нас души порыв)
> Утраченной привет любезный
> И радости былой отзыв.

> In the hour of twilight, that sacred hour,
> When dew is shedding coolness,
> I hasten to a lonely hill
> To watch the night sky.
> I dream, that from ethereal heights
> The recluses of the earthly land
> Are flying together to the lyre's sounds
> Hearing the songs of old times . . .
> And, giving freedom to [my] remembrance,
> I express by the play [music] of strings,
> How, [being full of] tender feelings toward enchantment,
> I was sharing [imparting] life with you,
> And I hear: from the aerial abyss
> (So strong is the soul's eruption)

A lost one's amiable regards
And an echo of past joy.[13]

Gogol's contribution to the elegiac genre comes not in poetry, but rather in his best known work, *Dead Souls*. This *poema,* which Gogol started in 1835 (he was writing and rewriting "The Nose" from 1832 to 1836, simultaneously with *Dead Souls*), we get into a gallery of noses, with different functions. Here, I am interested in one of these functions, which might be called causative, that is, leading to deprivation. Nose = loss. This is Gogol's personal code in *Dead Souls,* and, as we will see, this code will be present again in "The Nose."

Chichikov, whom Nabokov once labeled "a traveling salesman from Hades," might with equal right be called an elegiac man. Let us recall what he does in Gogol's "poem in prose." Chichikov buys "dead souls," that is, dead serfs. This activity would be completely compatible with the actions of the hero in Glebov's elegy, who calls together "recluses of the earthly land," now in "ethereal heights," to the sounds of his "lyre." In Chichikov's case, this would be his famous wallet-strongbox. In other words, Chichikov, when buying dead serfs, is collecting what is *lost*. In fact, the purpose of his activity is elegiac: he is buying dead people in order to fill the *emptiness* of his life and his *lonely* existence—we discover that Chichikov's life story is generally unhappy only in the last, eleventh chapter of the book, though hints at it abound earlier. Actually, Chichikov's inner world and peace are dependent on "the other world" almost as much as was in the case with Vasilii Zhukovsky, for whom ghosts were part of reality, and who wrote many elegies on this topic. Of course, as is always true in Gogol, all genres are made into a parody. Here, Chichikov is a parody of an elegiac hero, and much like Chichikov's strongbox this Gogolian parody has numerous levels and drawers.

After Chichikov's purchases of dead serfs from various landowners, he becomes a popular man in NN, the town where the action occurs. Naturally, no one in NN but those landowners from whom Chichikov is buying suspects that his serfs are already dead. Because Chichikov becomes fashionable, some unknown admirer sends him a letter:

> The letter opened decisively, in this manner to be exact: "Yes, I must write to you!" Then it went on to speak of a secret affinity of souls: that truth was punctuated with a number of dots which took up almost half a line. Next followed several reflections so remarkable for their justice that we consider it almost essential to quote them: 'What is our life? A valley where sorrow dwells. What is the world? A crowd of people who have no feelings.' Then the writer mentioned that she was bedewing the lines with tears for a tender mother, who departed this life some twenty-five years ago. Chichikov was asked to

find a refuge in the desert and to forsake forever the city where men suffocate for lack of air behind stifling barriers; the letter ended on a note of resolute despair and was rounded off with these verses:

> Two turtle doves will draw
> You to my chilly bier,
> And coo there till you saw
> That I died in tears.

The last line did not scan, but that did not matter: the letter was written in the spirit of those times. (chapter 8, p. 170)[14]

The opening line, "Yes, I must write to you!," is already a hint of a parody of Tatyana's famous love letter to Onegin from the third chapter of Pushkin's *Eugene Onegin* (the chapter was composed in 1824 and published in 1827). This letter starts: "I write to you—no more confession/is needed, nothing's left to tell./I know it's now in your discretion/with scorn to make my world a hell."[15] As is pointed out in Iurii Lotman's comments to *Eugene Onegin,* Pushkin modeled Tatyana's letter on an elegy of Marceline Desbordes-Valmore (1785–1859), a minor French poetess, whose elegiac collection of 1819 had been a success in France and in Russia.[16] In the lady's love letter to Chichikov, Gogol hints at Pushkin's novel in verse constantly. Thus, for example, "dots which took up almost half a line" after "a secret affinity of souls" ironically allude to Pushkin's hoaxing device of using dots in *Eugene Onegin* for absent line(s) and stanza(s) in order to make them look as if they were purposely removed by the author or extracted by the censorship. Phrases like "What is our life? A valley where sorrow dwells" mirror Batiushkov's popular comparison of human life to a "magic valley of tears" from his last "sane" poem of 1821: "Do you know what has said . . ." ("Ты знаешь, что изрек . . ."). They also reflect the poetic style of Pushkin's character Lensky, his well-known "bad elegy" full of generic clichés from *Eugene Onegin*'s sixth chapter (composed in 1826 and published in 1828):

> Whither, oh whither are ye banished,
> my golden days when spring was dear?
> What fate is my tomorrow brewing?
> the answer's past all human viewing,
> it's hidden deep in gloom and dust.
> No matter; fate's decree is just.
> Whether the arrow has my number,
> whether it goes careering past,
> all's well; the destined hour at last

> comes for awakening, comes for slumber;
> blessed are daytime's care and cark,
> blest is the advent of the dark!17

Lines about a lady's mother who died "some twenty-five years ago" are typical for the elegiac genre grievings about early death of someone who will never be forgotten. A call "to find refuge in the desert and to forsake forever the city" is an elegiac commonplace, known even from great poems, including Pushkin's "Poet" (1827), with its ending about the Romantic habit of running from the vanity of the world "to the shores of deserted waves, / to widely sounding forests" ("На берега пустынных волн, / В широкошумные дубровы . . ."). The letter, as Gogol puts it, "was written in the spirit of those times," and that spirit was elegiac. What is more, precisely this epistolary elegy becomes the force driving Chichikov to a ball, from which his fall starts. The only reason he goes there is to find the lady who wrote it.

At the ball, before Chichikov appears, the society of NN discusses his future and, in particular, his chances for finding a good steward for his newly bought serfs. What is especially interesting is that this discussion is couched in purely "nasal" terms:

> But the superintendent maintained that you could not get a good steward under five thousand roubles. The president objected that you could find one for three thousand. Whereupon the superintendent retorted: *"Where would you find him? Not under our nose, is he?"* To this the president replied: *"No, not under our nose, but right here in the district. . . ."* (chapter 8, p. 164; emphasis added)

Moreover, the ladies of the ball are also described by Gogol via their "nasal" functions:

> They could never be heard saying: "I blew my nose, I am perspiring, I spat." *Instead, they expressed themselves in this manner: "I relieved my nose" or "I had recourse to my handkerchief."* (chapter 8, p. 169; emphasis added)

Finally, Chichikov appears at the ball, where his pose, as Gogol depicts it, is that of one who is "nosing out" the lady letter writer:

> *Chichikov could only prick up his nose and sniff the scented air.* . . . As Chichikov stood facing them [the ladies], he was thinking to himself: "Now who could be the writer of that epistle?" *But as he thrust his nose out, it came up against a whole swirling battery of elbows, cuffs, sleeves, fragrant chemisettes and dresses.* (chapter 8, pp. 173, 174; emphasis added)

Not without interest is the fact that one of those people who surround Chichikov at this moment is "the Georgian prince Tchipkhaykhilidaev," a pun-name from *tchikhat'*, "to sneeze."

Gogol continues to surround Chichikov with noses, and soon after his arrival he falls in love with the governor's daughter. The love letter, written in terms of loss, as well as the gallery of noses, including Chichikov's own, decisively foreshadow his sudden loss in love. However, this loss is just a preview of the two that follow: Chichikov's loss of his reputation and . . . but about the last one I will speak later.

While Chichikov is still preoccupied with what for him are new feelings, his evil spirit Nozdrev appears. Nozdrev, we recall, not only refused to sell dead souls but also almost beat Chichikov to death. At the ball, Nozdrev stumbles upon Chichikov, who is up in the love-clouds, and starts to reveal to those present the truth about his serfs:

> 'Ah, you Kherson landowner, you Kherson landowner!' he was shouting as he approached, roaring with laughter till his cheeks, fresh and pink as a spring rose, quivered and shook. 'Well! Have you been doing a good trade in the dead ones? But you did not know, Your Excellency,' he yelled, turning to the governor, 'that he trades in dead souls. Honest, he does! Listen, Chichikov! I am telling you this out of friendship, we are all friends of yours here, and His Excellency is here too, I say I'd have you hanged. Upon my soul, I would!' (chapter 8, p. 183)

Chichikov is lost or, as Gogol puts it, he "simply did not know where he stood." Henceforth, the scandal around Chichikov snowballs and he feels it necessary to flee from NN. The most momentous thing for us here is not the moment from which Chichikov's fall starts but its cause—Nozdrev. Why?

In Russian, his name, as are almost all names in Gogol, is transparent and may be translated as Nostrilov, since it is derived from *nozdria*, "nostril." Thus, according to the nature of his name, Nozdrev-Nostrilov is already himself a "walking nose," who/which costs Chichikov his reputation. Moreover, Chichikov's name, though to a lesser extent, is talkative too: it somehow hints at the Russian verb *chikat'* (to beat, to cut, to stub) as well as the interjection *chik-chik*, often used instead of "to cut (off) something with a knife."[18] Chichikov's future as a landowner is cut off, so to speak, linguistically in advance, and he is cut off from society in accordance with the logic of his own name.

Thus, the relationship of Chichikov to Nozdrev recalls that of Kovalev to his nose. There is no physical scar here, but rather a psychological one. Chichikov comes to Nozdrev to buy dead souls, and the latter rejects him, whereas Kovalev approaches his nose, and the latter does not recognize him.

Nozdrev comes for Chichikov and Kovalev's nose returns to him. In any case, noses are involved directly in Chichikov's two losses, and Gogol continues to chase him with them until the very finale. In *Dead Souls,* Hamlet's famous motto "words, words, words" seems to metamorphose into "noses, noses, noses."

After the ball, rumors about Chichikov's dead souls go on and strike NN's officials, and again via the "nasal" metaphor:

> For a minute they found themselves in the position of a schoolboy *who in his sleep has had a "hussar" or a piece of paper filled with snuff thrust into his nose by his school fellows who were awake and up before him. In his sleep he takes a deep breath and draws in all the snuff, and then, on waking, jumps up, looks round him like an idiot with bulging eyes.* . . . (chapter 9, p. 202; emphasis added)

These rumors have been initiated by two ladies and, not surprisingly, what they found most offensive about Chichikov was his nose or, as Gogol portrays this situation: "They have started a rumor that he [Chichikov] is a fine fellow, *but he is not at all a fine fellow, not at all, and as for his nose . . . it's a nasty sight . . .*" (chapter 9, p. 195; emphasis added) What is more significant, Nozdrev-Nostrilov-The Nose, according to the same rumor, has been involved in Chichikov's nonexistent plan to kidnap the governor's daughter. In "Nevsky Prospect" the nose does not escape but is almost prepared to do so; in *Dead Souls,* Nozdrev-The Nose supposedly shares Chichikov's "intention" to organize some escape. Both situations look like spade-work for "The Nose."

Rumors about Chichikov reach even those landowners who never leave their countryside homes to visit NN. Their names, Zavalishin and Polezhaev, also talking and related to a few verbs with the meaning of "to lie (down)," are, in Gogol's description, "very popular with us in Russia, just as are the phrases 'to visit Sopikov' or 'to visit Khrapovitzky,' *which signify all forms of deadly sleepiness, on one's side, on one's back and in all other positions, accompanied by snores, nasal whistling and other exercises . . .*" (chapter 9, pp. 203–4; emphasis added) All these noses again!

All these noses fall down on Chichikov, tempting his already disturbed mind. Finally, after his reputation has already been lost, Chichikov—and this is a conclusive loss—almost loses his sanity. Gogol indicates: "Like a sleepwalker he wandered aimlessly about the town, unable to decide whether he was mad himself or whether the officials had gone off their heads, whether all this was a *dream* or whether this *nonsensical reality was stranger than fiction*" (chapter 10, p. 230; emphasis added). Moreover, the only one to visit Chichikov in this state is again Nozdrev—the nose, so to speak, returns to his own victim: "While Nozdrev was chattering away, Chichikov rubbed his eyes several times, wishing to make sure that *he was not dreaming*" (chapter 10, p. 232; emphasis added).

"The Nose" looks as if it were a sequel to this passage of *Dead Souls*:

> Kovalev the collegiate assessor woke up early next morning and made the sound "brrrr . . ." with his lips as he always did when he woke up, though he could not himself have explained the reason for his doing so. Kovalev stretched and asked for a little mirror that was standing on the table. He wanted to look at a pimple which had appeared on his nose the previous evening, but to his great astonishment there was a completely flat space where his nose should have been. Frightened, Kovalev asked for some water and a towel to rub his eyes; there really was no nose. *He began feeling with his hand, and pinched himself whether he was still asleep: it appeared that he was not*. The collegiate assessor jumped out of bed, he shook himself—there was still no nose . . . He ordered his clothes to be given him at once and flew off straight to the police commissioner [emphasis added].[19]

The "dream" and "nonsensical reality" between which the "mad" Chichikov tried to choose and which were interlaced with various noses and their unquestionable leader, Mr. Nostrilov in *Dead Souls,* bring us directly to "The Nose."

RETURN 2: NEW APPROACHES TO THE PLOT

It is well known that Gogol intended to title his story "The Dream" but then changed his mind. Why did he do this? "Dream" and "nose," respectively *son* and *nos* in Russian, form an obvious palindrome, which Gogol, I believe, found too cheap to allow. Or, equally probably, he simply did not want to make it easy for us to break his personal code. Still, the nose disappears in the morning *after* Kovalev's dream and returns to his face in the morning, too:

> Waking up and casually glancing into the mirror, he sees—his nose! puts up his hands—actually his nose! "Aha!" said Kovalev, and in his joy he almost danced a jig barefoot about his room; but the entrance of Ivan stopped him. He ordered Ivan to bring him water at once, and as he washed he glanced once more into the mirror—the nose! As he wiped himself with the towel he glanced into the mirror—the nose![20]

All events in "The Nose" take place within the brackets of these two awakenings.

In the 1910s another classic writer of the "nonsensical" starts his short story with a scene amazingly similar to Kovalev's awakening in Gogol:

As Gregor Samsa awoke one morning from a troubled dream he found himself transformed in his bed into a monstrous insect. He was lying on his hard, as it were armor-plated, back and when he lifted his head a little he could see his dome-like brown belly divided into corrugated segments on top of which the bed quilt could hardly keep in position and was about to slide off completely. His numerous legs, which were pitifully thin compared to the rest of his bulk, flimmered [*flicker + shimmer*] helplessly before his eyes. "What has happened to me? he thought. It was no dream . . ." [Nabokov's emphasis][21]

"The Metamorphosis" of Franz Kafka, with its after-dream absurdity and Gregor's death as an insect in its end, bears Gogol's touch, though it drastically differs from the Gogolian kind of absurdity, which yields to no logical interpretations.

In Kafka, we still can argue about whether its author's intentions were related to his wish to respond to the topic, also Gogolian, of the "little man" or, as Nabokov put it, to show the true "insects" among humans. But how should we interpret Gogol's pretense to write complete nonsense with no direct symbolism involved? In Kafka, the plot's development is linear: Gregor becomes an insect and dies as such; reality transforms into absurdity and stays that way. In Gogol, Kovalev's loss of his nose is a joke because he gets it back: it is an absurdity within a reality.

At the same time, a dream device does not help to deepen the conception of "The Metamorphosis," but it does excuse the events in "The Nose." We can speculate that Kovalev just had a bad dream about his nose's loss. Does this mean then that Gogol kept the dream device inside the narration and merely removed it from the title? The temptation to explain the story's plot as just a dream, of course, exists, though this is too easy and, furthermore, it was rejected by Gogol himself. The dead end of no(n)sense exists too, if one does not make a U-turn, which I intend to do right now. As Gogol himself puts it in the end of "The Nose," ". . . are there not absurd things everywhere?—and yet, when you think it over, there really is something in it." I believe, that a positive stress on "is" might help us in figuring out this concealed "something."

U-TURN: WHERE DO NOSES LIVE?

> *January, 28, 1836.* . . . We talked a lot about the imaginary discovery of the residents of the moon. Pushkin was arguing the absurdity of this idea, considering it an impertinent bluff, which it turned out to be later, and was laugh-

ing at the credulity of those who have a weakness for taking a bold fantasy at its face value.
—E. A. Drashusova, *Diary of the Unknown*[22]

In other writings of Gogol besides "The Nose," the role of a nose on the human face is twofold: a nose either works nearly as a vacuum cleaner that sucks into itself other parts of the face, or it *almost* disappears. For example, when in *Dead Souls* Chichikov meets the landowner Manilov again, sometime after their deal, Gogol depicts Manilov's face in the following way: "The kisses they [Manilov and Chichikov] showered on each other were so powerful that their front teeth ached for the rest of the day. Manilov's joy was so pronounced *that his nose and lips were all that remained of his face—his eyes disappeared entirely.*" (chapter 7, p. 146; emphasis added) Though the nose in this portrait is not a full champion and shares its "vacuum" functions with the lips, the whole picture nevertheless is a sort of limbering-up before a nose description that will take over a few pages later, in the image of another personage, Ivan Antonovich, a bureaucrat whom Chichikov meets in the "deeds section" *(krepostnaia ekspeditsiia)*: "He was well over forty, with black, thick hair; *the whole middle of his face jutted out and concentrated in his nose; in short, it was the sort of face that is commonly known as a 'jug snout.'*" (chapter 7, p. 151; emphasis added) Here, the nose is the sole face-survivor and becomes its plenipotentiary ambassador to Gogol's world.

As for the nose's second role—its disappearance—this never occurs in full before "The Nose," but only half-happens, as we have already seen in "Nevsky Prospect." Even Nozdrev-Nostrilov, who *is* a "walking nose," is not a fully independent one, being bound with his human hypostasis, and there are more "half-autonomous" noses like him in *Dead Souls*. Thus, for example, when rumors about Chichikov's bargain arise, at a certain point somebody recalls an incident with the merchants who have visited NN. These merchants gave a party which, of course, ended in a big fight: "One of the triumphant band had his 'snout knocked off,' as the champions put it, that is to say, *it was squashed to such a degree that there was hardly a trace of it left on his face.*" (chapter 9, p. 207; emphasis added) "Hardly a trace," as Gogol puts it here, transforms into "no trace at all" in "The Nose." Major Kovalev's face, without a nose, famously becomes "as flat as a pancake," while a nose starts its separate existence.

Simultaneously with "The Nose," in 1833 and 1834, Gogol wrote "The Diary of a Madman," which in 1835 he would include in the collection *Arabesques*. There, in Poprishchin's diary, which mirrors this hero's step-by-step descent into lunacy, on pages marked by the impossible date "February Thirtieth," we read:

Tomorrow at seven o'clock a strange event will occur: the earth will land on moon. The famous English chemist Weelington has written about this. I confess that I felt my heart tremble when I thought about the unusual softness and fragility of the moon. The moon, you know, is usually made in Hamburg; and very badly made as well. I find it surprising that England has paid any attention to all this. A lame cooper makes it and it's obvious that the fool doesn't know a thing about the moon. He mixed in a tarred rope and one part of lamp-oil; and that's why there's such an awful smell over the whole earth that it's necessary to bung up one's nose. *And because of this the moon itself is such a tender ball that people could never live on it, and now only a few noses live there. And it's for that same reason that we cannot see our own noses, because they're all on the moon.* And when I thought of how heavy an article the world is and how it would grind our noses into flour, then I was overcome with such anxiety that, putting on my socks and shoes, I dashed into the hall of the state council with the intention of ordering the police not to let the earth land on the moon [emphasis added].[23]

The idea of noses living on the moon is only partially nonsensical, for the connection between noses separated from "their" faces and the moon may be metaphorical. When giving the "abnormal" answer that noses live on the moon instead of the normal one that they live on the face, Gogol is reusing a poetic cliché, nourished by many cultures and literary movements. A comparison of a face to the moon is as old as the Song of Solomon ("Who is she that looketh forth as the morning, fair as the moon . . . ," Song of Sol. 6:10) or Arabic literature, in which authors liken the lover's face to it.[24] By the time of Romanticism this simile was already a banality.

The metaphor of Kovalev's face looking like a pancake (*blin* in Russian) is far more fascinating. In Russia, pancakes are the ritual food during Shrovetide week (*maslenitsa*), just before Lent. In pre-Christian times, the same week was the celebration of the early spring, connected to the moon's phases, namely its revival, the new moon.[25] Face-moon-baking is, therefore, a metaphorical triad in Gogol (it must be noted that in Russian one verbally bakes rather than fries pancakes—*pech' blini* is the expression). Generally, however, this triad is represented with an ellipsis, by only two of its parts. In *Dead Souls,* for example, we read that some of Chichikov's former colleagues "had faces like badly-baked loaves of bread" (chapter 11, p. 249). The triad is thus represented by "face" and "baking." In "The Diary of a Madman," these parts are "face," "nose" as its synecdoche, and "moon"; in "The Nose"—"face" and "baking" (pancake) again. It is noteworthy that Gogol uses almost the same words when he typifies these parts. In "The Diary of a Madman," the moon is "badly made," and in *Dead Souls* faces are "badly-baked." The fact that the nose, the Gogolian synecdoche of the *face,* gets into the barber's *bread* in "The Nose" looks less unmotivated if we keep this triad in mind.

Still, the sense of noses' fragility, the fear that the earth will "grind our noses into flour," is not less impressive in Poprishchin's diary than his idea of noses living on the moon. Are they made of glass? In any case, the noses' existence on the moon is linked to their fragility a strange way.

RETURN 3: PANCAKE OR A PUNCAKE?

> Moreover, gentlemen, there is every reason to fear
> that, if we neglect the worship of the gods,
> they will split us up again, and then we
> shall have to go about with our noses sawed
> asunder, part and counterpart, like the basso-
> relievos on the tombstones.
> —Plato, *Symposium* (193 a)[26]

In his never-completed *Textbook of Literature for Russian Youth (Uchebnaia kniga slovesnosti dlia russkogo iunoshestva)*, whose idea goes back to the 1830s and which was probably drafted in 1845, Gogol intended to show his unique approach to the different genres of literature and to establish their hierarchy. After 1840, he planned a second part of *Dead Souls* and therefore discourses in his manual on the epic, in particular on what he calls "a minor epic," and does so with some thoroughness. Gogol states: "There is no possibility of universality, but full epic quantity of some outstanding local occurrences exists and can exist, as long as the poet clothes it in verse. Thus, Ariosto lent fairytale passion to adventures and to the fantastic, with which the entire epoch was preoccupied for a while. . . ."[27] Together with Ariosto, Gogol names only Cervantes as a representative of the minor epic. For the major epic he chooses Homer.

It is well known that Gogol, almost like Alexander of Macedonia long before him, never parted with *The Iliad* and tried to recapture its stylistic spirit in his own epic "Taras Bulba." The fact that Gogol names Ariosto right after Homer and even before Cervantes seems a sort of "outstanding local occurrence," too, but it is not incidental. In Gogol's time, Ludovico Ariosto (1474–1533), the Renaissance Italian poet and the author of *Orlando Furioso* (1532), a gigantic epic poem of forty-six cantos, was immensely popular in Russia. Pieces of his epic were translated by Alexander Pushkin, Konstantin Batiushkov, Pavel Katenin (1792–1853), and Ivan Kozlov (1779–1840). However, the most famous and full translation of *Orlando Furioso* belongs to the less remembered but then influential Semen Raich (1792–

Writing as Exorcism

1855). It was published from 1832 to 1837, precisely the years of Gogol's work on "The Nose" and his thinking about his *Textbook of Literature for Russian Youth,* in which Ariosto was given a major place.[28]

The reason that Ariosto's epic was picked up by Russian Romanticism is understandable: *Orlando Furioso* is simultaneously exceptionally heroic *and* fantastic, and thus represents the closest approach in classic literature to the dual "Schiller-Hoffmann" Romantic mode, ironically captured by Gogol in "Nevsky Prospect."

Its heroic plot is based upon the story of a famous knight, Orlando, who, being in love with the lady Angelica and having heard about her betrayal, goes mad and starts behaving like an animal. Orlando's friend Astolpho, also a great knight, wants to help him, and this is where the epic's fantastic side, noted by Gogol, becomes particularly strong. In order to save Orlando, Astolpho goes to the terrestrial paradise, in which he meets St. John, who tells him the following (canto XXXIV, LXV–LXVII):[29]

> "Hence God hath made him mad, and, in this vein,
> "Belly, and breast, and naked flank expose;
> "And so diseased and troubled is his brain,
> "That none, at least himself, the champion knows.
> "Nebuchadnezzar whilom to such pain
> "God in his vengeance doomed, as story shows;
> "Sent, for seven years, of savage fury full,
> "To feed on grass and hay, like slavering bull.
>
> "But yet, because the Christian paladine
> "Has sinned against his heavenly Maker less,
> "He only for three months, by will divine,
> "Is doomed to cleanse himself of his excess.
> "Nor yet with other scope did your design
> "Of wending hither the Redeemer bless,
> "But that through us the mode you should explore,
> "Orlando's missing senses to restore."

But what should Astolpho do? The answer is an odd one: he must go to the moon.

> "'Tis true to journey further ye will need,
> "And wholly must you leave this nether sphere;
> "To the *moon's circle* you have to lead,
> "Of all the planets to our world most near.

"Because the medicine, that is fit to speed
"Insane Orlando's cure, is treasured here.
"This night will we away, when over head
"Her downward rays the silver moon shall shed [emphasis added]."

Why exactly should Astolpho go to the moon? According to Ariosto's fantastic map, it is the place where lost human minds are kept in various vases and flasks (now we would probably say in test tubes or measuring cups). Thus, Astolpho travels to the moon in a special "chariot" and reaches the place where he finds Orlando's mind (canto XXXIV, LXXXIII–LXXXV):

It was as 'twere a liquor soft and thin,
Which, save well corked, would from the vase have drained;
Laid up, and treasured various flasks within,
Larger or lesser, to that use ordained.
That largest was which of the paladin,
Anglantes' lord, the mighty sense contained;
And from those others was discerned, since writ
Upon the vessel was ORLANDO'S WIT.

The names of those wits therein were pent
He thus on all those other flasks espied.
Much of his own, but with more wonderment,
The sense of many others he descried,
Who, he believed, no dram of theirs had spent;
But here, by tokens clear was satisfied,
That scantily therewith were they purveyed;
So large the quantity he here surveyed.

Some waste on love, some seeking honour, lose
Their wits, some, scowering seas, for merchandise,
Some, that on wealthy lords their hope repose,
And some, befooled by silly sorceries;
These upon pictures, upon jewels those;
These on whatever else they highest prize.
Astrologers' and sophists' wits mid these,
And many a poet's too, Astolpho sees.

After Orlando's mind is found in a vase Astolpho takes it back to the earth. In the next, seventh volume of Ariosto's epic, after various adventures

Writing as Exorcism

he brings the vase to Orlando. Orlando resists Astolpho's cure, but the latter, with other paladins helping him, finally succeeds (canto XXXIX, LVI–LVII):

> Seven times Astolpho makes them [the other knights] wash the knight;
> And seven times plunged beneath the brine he goes.
> So that they cleanse away the scurf and blight,
> Which to his stupid limbs and visage grows.
> This done, with herbs, for that occasion dight,
> *They stop his mouth, wherewith he puffs and blows.*
> *For, save his nostrils, would Astolpho leave*
> *No passage whence the count might air receive.*
>
> Valiant Astolpho had prepared the vase,
> Wherein Orlando's senses were contained,
> *And to his nostrils in such mode conveys,*
> *That, drawing-in his breath, the county drained*
> *The mystic cup withal. Oh wondrous case!*
> The unsettled mind its ancient seat regained;
> And, in its glorious reasonings, yet more clear
> And lucid waxed his wisdom than whilere [emphasis added].

The scene of bringing the vase with Orlando's mind back to Orlando by Astolpho does not directly recall but then somehow corresponds with the fact of Kovalev's nose being brought back to him by the policeman. The latter says Kovalev's nose was caught at the border, but with the same "motivation" it could have been caught on the moon. Moreover, the fact of a nose that is back but is separated from Kovalev's face corresponds to the many difficulties Astolpho goes through in order to put Orlando's mind back into its owner's head. Kovalev asks a doctor to put his nose back in his face but is refused. Also, both Orlando's mind and Kovalev's nose are back after, or before, some, so to speak, water treatment: Orlando is cleaned from "the scurf and blight" and then drinks the stuff while his nostrils are held by Astolpho; Kovalev is ready to wash his face, then suddenly finds his nose in its former place, and a pimple is "cleaned away," too. Both cases are "wondrous" indeed. However, these parallels would still remain far-fetched if not for another common dimension.

Magnifying Glass 1

In "Nevsky Prospect," Schiller and Hoffmann are both drunk and *are going out of their minds in connection with a nose.*

Magnifying Glass 2

In *Dead Souls,* various noses chase Chichikov, tempting his already disturbed mind. Finally, after his reputation is already lost, *he, for a while, loses his sanity.*

Magnifying Glass 3

Poprishchin, who sends noses to live on the moon, *is* a madman.

In Gogol, as is visible through three "magnifying glasses," noses either lead to insanity of various kinds or are connected to it. In Ariosto, as is clear from three quoted fragments, lost minds, including Orlando's, are kept on the moon; also, they can be brought back, and a nose (nostrils) participates in the process of getting the lost mind back. How does all this help to understand "The Nose"?

Gogol's change of the story's title from "The Dream" *(son)* to "The Nose" *(nos)*, probably because the palindrome in the title looks too uncovered, nevertheless does not deny the possibility of another pun at the story's pivot. If Gogol thought about it in the first place, why would he change his mind? What is the pun?

And here is the oven in which Gogol's "puncake" is baked. "Nose" *(nos)* and "mind" also form a pun if we recall that "mind" in phonetic Greek is *nus* (νοῦς). As a person who had graduated from a high school in the Russian Empire *(gimnaziia),* Gogol could not have escaped at least some knowledge of Greek and Latin. It is certain that this important word, essential for ancient philosophy, was part of his vocabulary. As a person with a sharp linguistic ear, Gogol might have also imagined this *nus,* which, according to Aristotle, is the prime mover of our universe, as a big "nose," existing out there. Moreover, taking into consideration the fact that Kovalev's first name is Platon—that is, Plato in Russian—Gogol's play on words becomes even more convenient: he substituted Aristotle for Plato, about whom Gogol thought frequently. Thus, in the lecture and essay "Al-Mamun," which Gogol read in 1834 and included in his collection *Arabesques* of 1835, we find Gogol's characterization of Aristotle as "the all-embracing and exacting philosopher of Greece." Moreover, Gogol writes:

> Arab scholars, long occupied with the sluggish work, had already become attracted to exactness and formality [of Aristotle] and thus became absorbed in it with erudite enthusiasm. These endless conclusions, the bringing of a sense of order and outward appearance to what had previously only existed

in their souls like fiery remnants, could not but enchant the scholars of the day.³⁰

Though Plato himself did not pay as much attention to the concept of νοῦς as did Aristotle, the Platonists, especially Plotinus, developed it later into the axis of their theory. Curiously enough, the Russian *nos* is immured in this philosopher's name: *Plôtinos* (Πλωτῖνος). Kovalev of "The Nose"—for two weeks, like Chichikov for a few days—loses his *nus,* his mind, and thus all reality surrounding him becomes no(n)sense, compatible with the "fantastic" in *Orlando Furioso.* Kovalev is thus the most logical and parodic conclusion to Gogol's gallery of madmen by the fault of a nose.

RETURN 4: WHAT DID GOGOL ENCODE
IN "THE NOSE"?

> *Mayor.* . . . What they say is true, "Those
> whom God wishes to destroy, He first deprives
> of reason [*razum*]."
> —Gogol, *The Inspector General*

Though initially "The Nose" was intended for *Moskovskii Nabliudatel' (The Moscow Spectator),* it was first published in 1836 in Pushkin's magazine *Sovremennik (Contemporary),* in its third issue. Pushkin accompanied the publication with his own note: "N. V. Gogol for a long time did not agree to publish this joke; but we found in it such a great deal that was unexpected, fantastic, cheerful, original, that we persuaded him to allow us to share with the public the pleasure his manuscript gave us."³¹

Gogol was introduced to Pushkin in May 1831 (Pushkin had just returned to Petersburg from Moscow, where he had married Nataliia Goncharova).³² For Gogol, their relation became definitive: Pushkin was his key to the literary world. Gogol, in his turn, at least in his own words, was the definitive force behind Pushkin's decision to start *Sovremennik* in 1836. In his letter of 1846 to Pletnev, the journal's chief editor after Pushkin's death in 1837, Gogol recalls: "However, a strong wish to publish this magazine [*Sovremennik*] did not exist in him [Pushkin], and he did not expect any great good from it. Given permission to start it, he was about to turn the whole thing down. I take the blame upon myself: I talked him into it. I promised to be a faithful contributor."³³

Pushkin's influence on Gogol's work was enormous. As he pointed out in his "Author's Confession" ("Avtorskaiia ispoved'") of 1847,

Gogol's Nausea and Nossea

> The reason for the cheerfulness, noticed in my first published writings, lay in some spiritual need. Attacks of depression, which I failed to explain, were coming over me, perhaps, because of my unhealthy condition. In order to entertain myself, I started inventing as much that was funny as I could. . . . Probably, with age and with less need to entertain myself this cheerfulness would have disappeared by itself, and my creative writing together with it. But Pushkin forced me to look at this matter seriously. . . . And in conclusion, he gave me his own topic [*siuzhet*], on which he intended to do a sort of long narrative poem [*poema*] and which, according to his own words, he would never give to anybody else. It was the topic of *Dead Souls*. (The idea of *The Inspector General* also belongs to him.)[34]

What is noteworthy here besides the direct recognition of Pushkin's influence is Gogol's confession of having had attacks of depression, which he overcame with the help of his own creativity, and the way he links their disappearance with Pushkin's name.

In 1852, Gogol's physician Tarasenkov started talking with him about "The Diary of a Madman." "After telling him that I constantly deal with psychopaths and even own their genuine diaries, I wished to know from him whether he had read such diaries before he wrote this story. He answered: 'Read, but later.'—'But how did you draw then so realistically?'—I asked him. 'It is easy: one just has to imagine. . . .'"[35]

Nor was the recreation of madness solely a literary game for Gogol. According to his school comrades, the future author, while still in Nezhin, twice imitated madness and very successfully: once in order to avoid punishment, and the second time to get more leisure for his writing.[36]

Doubtless, Gogol's predisposition to mental disorder, based on his ability to imagine things and even imitate insanity, might have been torturing. In 1843 and 1844, Gogol wrote a treatise, "On Those of Our Mental Predispositions and Defects That Embarrass Us and Prevent Us from Being Calm" ("O tekh dushevnykh raspolozheniiakh i nedostatkakh nashykh, kotorye proizvodiat v nas smushchenie i meshaiiut nam prebyvat' v spokoinom sostoianii"). One of its chapters he titles "On Anxiety, Hypochondria and Lack of Confidence" ("O boiazni, mnitel'nosti i neuverennosti v sebe"). In this chapter, Gogol tries to exorcise all three by God's word, that is, the New Testament. He writes:

> All three come from the fact that we are not strong still in major rules and laws, which only reading of The New Testament and Holy books can give us. Until we do not go deeper in the meaning of gospel truth, until we do not start addressing our love more to God than to the earth, till then major and minor, important and petty will continue to be mixed up in our heads . . .[37]

The treatise was written in the same years as *The Textbook of Literature for Russian Youth,* in which Gogol discusses "major and minor" as well, though in terms of literature (to recall, Ariosto there was declared the model for a minor epic), and before the "Author's Confession," in which Pushkin's role in Gogol's life was declared to be major.

As we noted in the previous chapter, between 1831 to 1837, from the year of his marriage till the year of his death, Pushkin suffered—almost constantly—from unremitting melancholia. Exactly these years cover the period in which Pushkin and Gogol knew each other. Ultimately, the strain that manifested itself in 1831 grew progressively worse until Pushkin's breakdown in 1836. Thus, one of his contemporaries wrote in 1831: "I recall how he when visiting us would walk sadly around the room . . . repeating in melancholia: 'I am dejected! what gloom!' . . . I am sure that all these worries for the future of his family, his debts, and constant concerns for living were the major reason for the bitterness he showed in the events that led to his death."[38] In 1833, Pushkin wrote to his wife from the estate in Boldino: "Yesterday, I felt such grief, that I even cannot remember when gloom like this came over me. . . . The past few days I had a constant headache, and gloom was eating me. Now it is better. I began many projects, but don't want to pursue anything; God knows what's happening with me."[39] That same year in Boldino, Pushkin wrote: "Please, God, do not let me go insane. / Yes, even a crook and a beggar-bag are less heavy; / Yes, even labor and hunger are less unbearable." The entire poem sounds like a kind of Pushkinian exorcism of his own life in its last period.

DIGRESSION 4: PUSHKIN'S ARIOSTO

What is more, in the same year and place (his Boldino estate) Pushkin composed *The Bronze Horseman,* a long narrative poem that touches upon his own comprehension of Peter the Great's historical role, the historical mission of the city of St. Petersburg, and the topic of the harmless "little man" versus the mighty state. However, what interests me about *The Bronze Horseman* here is the theme of madness chasing Eugene, the poem's protagonist. After the depiction of the disastrous flood of 1824, which washed away a good deal of the city, Eugene, one of the survivors, sails to one of Petersburg's many islands in order to find his fiancée Parasha. Not able even to find her house—it was also washed away by the flood—Eugene goes mad. Pushkin describes this moment and Eugene's life as a lunatic:

> Where is the house? Distraught and somber,
> He paces back and forward there,

> Talks to himself aloud, soon after
> Bursts out abruptly into laughter
> And slaps his forehead. . . .
> My pitiful Eugene, though—evil
> His lot; alas, his clouded mind
> Could not withstand the brute upheaval
> Just wrought on it. The clash and strain
> Of flood and storm forever thundered
> Upon his ear; his thoughts a train
> Of horrors, wordlessly he wandered;
> Some secret vision seemed to chill
> His mind. A week—a month—and still
> Astray from home he roved and pondered.
> As for the homestead he forsook,
> The landlord let his vacant nook
> To some poor poet. Eugene never
> Returned to claim it back, nor took
> His left possessions. Growing ever
> More alien to the world, he strayed
> All day on foot till nightfall led him
> Down to the wharves to sleep. He made
> His meals of morsels people fed him
> Through windows. His poor clothing frayed
> And moldered off him. Wicked urchins
> Threw pebbles at his back. The searching
> Coachwhips not seldom struck him when,
> As often now, he would be lurching
> Uncertain of his course; but then
> He did not feel it for the pain
> Of some loud anguish in his brain.
> Thus he wore on his luckless span,
> A moot thing, neither beast nor man,
> Who knew if this world's child, or whether
> A caller from the next. . . . [40]

In *Orlando Furioso* (canto XXIII), Orlando loses his mind when he discovers that Angelica has been unfaithful to him with Medoro. Medoro wrote a poem about their love, which Orlando—now—reads (CXI):

> Three times, and four, and six, the lines imprest
> Upon the stone that wretch perused, in vain
> Seeking another sense than was exprest,

Writing as Exorcism

> And ever saw the thing more clear and plain;
> And all the while, within his troubled breast,
> He felt an icy hard his heart-core strain.
> With mind and eyes close fastened on the block,
> At length he stood, not differing from the rock.

The similarity between the way the sudden onset of madness is presented in Pushkin and in Ariosto is striking. What is more, Orlando's escape from reality to the strange life of somebody who is "neither beast nor man" is echoed in *The Bronze Horseman* as well. In Ariosto's stanzas CXXIV–CXXV we read:

> In him, forthwith, such deadly hatred breed
> That bed, that house, that swain, he will not stay
> Till the morn break, or till the dawn succeed,
> Whose twilight goes before approaching day.
> In haste, Orlando takes his arms and steed;
> And to the deepest greenwood wends his way.
> And, when assured that he is there alone,
> Gives utterance to his grief in shriek and groan.
>
> Never from tears, never from sorrowing,
> He paused; nor found he peace by night or day:
> He fled from town, in forest harbouring,
> And in the open air on hard earth lay.
> He marvelled at himself, how such a spring
> Of water from his eyes could stream away,
> And breath was for so many sobs supplied;
> And thus ofttimes, amid his mourning, cried. . . .

Finally, "impelled by frenzy, the fourth day, / He from his limbs tore plate and mail away." Eugene also escapes from the city and eventually is found dead on "a little island," which "lies off the coast."

What is more, in 1826 Pushkin had started his own version of *Orlando Furioso,* and the piece he chose for translation is from canto XXIII, the same one in which Orlando loses his mind:

> Два, три раза, и пять, и шесть
> Он хочет надпись перечесть;
> Несчастный силится напрасно
> Сказать, что нет того, что есть.
> Он правду видит, видит ясно,
> И нестерпимая тоска,

Как бы холодная рука,
Сжимает сердце в нем ужасно,
И наконец на свой позор
Вперил он равнодушный взор.

Twice, three more times, and five, and six
He wants to read the inscription;
The wretch tries in vain
To say that what exists does not.
He sees the truth, sees it clearly,
And an unbearable gloom,
As if a cold hand,
Squeezes his heart terribly,
And finally upon his disgrace
He fastened his indifferent gaze.

Though Pushkin's version is amazingly close to the original (compare it to the English translation, which I have already quoted), there is no doubt that what Pushkin describes here is not just Orlando's state but his own frame of mind. Why? Pushkin went through a first real strain, comparable to the already described one of 1831 to 1836, in 1826, in the aftermath of the Decembrist uprising. That year, he felt himself hanging by a thread, wondering whether his place would be in Siberia, together with the Decembrists. He wanted to hope for the best but feared that he was only fooling himself, while madness might come in an instant, as it did to Orlando, who, like Eugene later, "sees the truth," and whose look then becomes "indifferent."

Furthermore, Pushkin wrote his *Orlando* in 1826, the same year that his friend and former mentor Batiushkov, completely insane since 1821, produced his last known poem, "Monument"—a version of Horace's ode, first adopted by Lomonosov and then by Derzhavin. Batiushkov, as I noted earlier, was one of the first to introduce Ariosto and Tasso to Russia. Ten years later, in 1836, Pushkin created his own version of Horace's-Lomonosov's-Derzhavin's-Batiushkov's "Monument"—"Я памятник себе воздвиг нерукотворный. . . ." There are too many coincidences to disregard Italian influence on the theme of madness in Pushkin. And if it was not that direct, then, at least, Pushkin's fear of madness is evident from the quoted pieces.

RETURN 5: GOGOL'S CONCEALED EXORCISM

It is impossible to prove whether Gogol knew these poems (considering his frequent meetings with Pushkin, he probably did), but it is certain that he was aware of Pushkin's mood of 1831 to 1836. Moreover, Gogol's own mental state was not better. Still, exactly in this shape he wrote *The Inspector General* and "The Nose" and started *Dead Souls*.

As for *The Inspector General,* we already know that Gogol said he encoded in it his own fears of God's punishment. In "The Nose," I believe, Gogol was rewriting, or, rather, developing Pushkin's (and his own) fears of going mad, as he did with Pushkin's ideas for *The Inspector General* and *Dead Souls*. At the same time, Gogol, developing Pushkin, tries—as before and after—to bring to this process various and already proven models. Thus, writing "Taras Bulba," Gogol was rewriting Homer; writing *Dead Souls,* he was rewriting both Homer and Dante. Writing "The Nose," Gogol rewrote *Orlando Furioso:* in the lost *nos* of Major Kovalev he fears to lose his own *nus;* he knows that to catch it on the Russian border is still possible, but to return it from the moon, after the *nus* is completely lost, would be impossible. Taking into consideration the fact that the nose as such is Gogol's favorite, most feared for, and most fragile part, then the mind's fragility—its existence, in Orlando's case, in a glass vial—must have been very disturbing for him. In Gogol's case, nose and mind, *nos* and *nus,* are tautological units, and losing one is automatically connected to the loss of the other. Pushkin's influence, like Pushkin's fears, is no less part of Gogol's life as of his creativity. As an exorcist, when writing about various types of madness, Gogol probably believed that if they were fixed on paper they would never occur in his real life.

To sum up, Pushkin's Eugene in *The Bronze Horseman,* Pushkin's Orlando, and Pushkin's "Italian" mentor Batiushkov all lost their minds and never got them back. In Gogol, who constantly wanted to be recognized as Pushkin's direct heir, Kovalev does get his nose/mind back from the policeman, as did Orlando who got it from Astolpho's hands. It looks as if Gogol—by describing the mind's fantastic recovery in his literary works—tried to prevent its loss in his real life. That is why Gogol's nossea is an overt life-fear of losing his *nus,* while his literary no(n)sense seems to be a kind of concealed exorcism of this phobia.

LAST DIGRESSION

On May 5, 1997, *Time* published an article, "Anatomy of Melancholy," about a sensational scientific discovery:

> It may turn out to be the most detailed snapshot ever taken of the depressed mind, showing where melancholy is mapped on the grey matter of the brain. Writing in last week's *Nature,* Drevets and his co-workers reported that they had zeroed in on a *tiny, thimble-size nodule of the brain located about 2.5*

inches behind the bridge of the nose. Other scientists had already shown that this section of the brain, called the subgenual prefrontal cortex, plays an important role in the control of emotions. But Drevets . . . discovered that it could also be a trigger point for both bouts of paralyzing sadness and the wildly euphoric highs of manic depression. "This area of the brain may act as a set of brakes for emotional responses," he explains. "When it does not function properly, abnormal swings in mood may occur" [emphasis added].

I cannot judge how scientific this claim is, but I swear that it sounds truly Gogolian.

Chapter Four

Rome before Rome

> Nihil est in rebus, quod ante non fuerit in verbis.
>
> There is nothing in the content that would not have been in the word before.
> —A. Peshkovsky
>
> The role of the city of Rome in Gogol's life is not thoroughly explored yet.
> —P. Annenkov

ROME LOST

Nikolai Gogol's exorcism is rich in variations. Mostly, as has been shown in the previous chapter, through writing, he was attempting to neutralize his worst fears—in particular the fear of losing his mind—and thus to prevent his "demons" from coming true. In this chapter I will try to unveil one more Gogolian exorcism, one that can be called an exorcism with complications because of its connection with another facet of Gogol's personality—his fatalism. Gogol's specific brand of fatalism took the form of a belief that good things in life, not just bad ones, can be directly influenced by words: words, in this view, do not describe reality; rather they create it. To put it a little bit differently, words for Gogol were either the magnet of life events or an antagonizing force; the latter we have already called his "nausea/nossea" in chapter 3. And, as usual, Gogol camouflages both categories. Why? Most probably, Gogol's coded intentions were connected to his major superstition: when magnetizing his destiny, he was afraid that its "all-seeing eye," to which we come later, would scare all the good things away and to avoid this everything needed to be very well hidden.

The reader of this chapter will find out how Gogol—on paper—already tried to predict, that is, to magnetize his Italian period when writing works set in Ukraine. Moreover, it will be shown how, in trying to attract this particular change in his life, Gogol was simultaneously struggling with his phobias.

Although most scholars describe "Ganz Küchelgarten" as Gogol's debut work, his actual first publication was a lyric poem. It appeared unobserved on March 23, 1829, in the then already right-wing magazine *Son of the Fatherland (Syn Otechestva)* under the title "Italy."[1] Unlike "Ganz Küchelgarten," "Italy" is surprisingly free of prosodic flaws, though it possesses an equally featureless Romanticism (the only oddness of the poem might be considered the line "Любовь роскошная веснует"—"voluptuous love springtimes"). The poem starts:

> Италия—роскошная страна!
> По ней душа и стонет и тоскует.
> Она вся рай, вся радости полна,
> И в ней любовь роскошная веснует.
> Бежит, шумит задумчиво волна
> И берега чудесные целует;
> В ней небеса прекрасные блестят;
> Лимон горит и веет аромат. . . .[2]

> Italy—voluptuous country!
> The soul pines for it and moans.
> It is all a paradise, all full of joy,
> And voluptuous love springtimes in it.
> Waves run and roll dreamily
> And kiss the marvelous shores;
> In it, the beautiful firmament glows;
> Lemons shine and scent the air. . . .

And concludes:

> Узрю ль тебя я, полный ожиданий?
> Душа в лучах, и думы говорят,
> Меня влечет и жжет твое дыханье,—
> Я в небесах, весь звук и трепетанье! . . .

> Full of expectation, shall I see you?
> My soul is in the rays, and thoughts speak,
> Your breath draws and burns me,—
> I am in heaven, I am all sound and quivering! . . .

Although it may have been consequential personally for Gogol, this opus did not make any difference for the poetic cult of Italy in Romantic-era

Russia. Poems about Italy were legion. For example, just a year before his untimely demise (that is, three years before Gogol's poem was published) another and far more confident Romantic, Dmitry Venevitinov (1805–27), wrote a poem titled "Italy":

> Италия, отчизна вдохновенья!
> Придет мой час, когда удастся мне
> Любить тебя с восторгом наслажденья,
> Как я люблю твой образ в светлом сне.
> Без горя я с мечтами распрощаюсь,
> И наяву, в кругу твоих чудес,
> Под яхонтом сверкающих небес,
> Младой душой по воле разыграюсь. . . .³

> Italy, fatherland of·inspiration!
> The time will come when I manage
> To love you with an ecstasy of enjoyment,
> As much as I love your image in my bright dreams.
> Without regret I will bid farewell to my fantasies
> And in reality, in the circle of your wonders,
> Beneath the sapphire of your glowing firmament
> My young soul will play freely.

The Romantic argot of Gogol's poem coincides with Venevitinov's "Italy" almost verbatim. In both (and this rhetoric is typical for many contemporary poems about the country), Italy stands for a land with a "glowing firmament"; it is a country of (in Gogol) and for (in Venevitinov) the soul. For both poets, this ideal country *must* one day be reached. As it happens, both poems are derived from the same progenitor—Goethe's poetic cycle "Mignon" of 1794. There, Italy stands for the same ideal goal-country, where "lemons bloom" ("Zitronen blühn"; in Gogol, "lemons shine") and "a soft wind blows from the blue sky" ("Ein sanfter Wind vom blauen Himmel weht"). Mignon's call, among the most famous in Romantic poetry, to disappear into that land of paradise forever ("Dahin! Dahin / Möcht ich mit dir, o mein Geliebter, ziehn") foreshadows Gogol's lines that Italy's "breath draws and burns" and that his "soul pines for it and moans," as well as Venevitinov's idea that one day he will find himself there forever.

In 1821, that is, five years before Venevitinov and eight before Gogol, another Russian poet, far less dependent on the Romantic clichés than others, Evgeny Baratynsky (1800–44), wrote a meditative poem, "Rome." His poem is elegiac and somehow nostalgic; it is about the historical, lost Rome, and there is no trace of the expected sweetness on the topic. Baratynsky's Romantic intonation is rather metallic, like a gait of a Roman legionnaire.

Rome before Rome

> Ты был ли, гордый Рим, земли самовластитель,
>   Ты был ли, о свободный Рим?
>   К немым развалинам твоим
> Подходит с грустию их чуждый навеститель.
> За что утратил ты величье прежных дней?
> За что, державный Рим, тебя заыли боги?
>   Град пышный, где твои чертоги?
> Где сильные твои, о родина мужей?[4]

> Were you, proud Rome, the ruler of the earth,
>   Were you, oh free Rome?
>   To your dumb ruins
> The alien visitor comes with sorrow.
> Why did you lose the glory of the old days?
> Why, sovereign Rome, did the gods forsake you?
>   Grand city, were are your mansions?
> Where are your mighty, oh motherland of men?

Almost nothing in Baratynsky's practice would have suggested that twenty-something years later he would exchange this masculine vigor for a dull Romantic lollipop. But that is precisely what happened, when, just a year before his death in 1844, Baratynsky wrote another poem on Italy. This time, we can find the whole set of well-worn Romantic clichés such as the poet's soul "bursting" in relation to Italy, Goethe-like "dreams" about the land's beauty, and so forth.

> Небо Италии, небо Торквата,
> Прах поэтический древнего Рима,
> Родина неги, славой богата,
> Будешь ли некогда мною ты зрима?
> Рвется душа, нетерпеньем объята,
> К гордым остаткам падшего Рима!
> Снятся мне долы, леса благовонны,
> Снятся упадших чертогов колонны! [5]

> Sky of Italy, sky of Torquato [Tasso],
> Poetic ashes of ancient Rome,
> Motherland of the voluptuousness, rich in glory,
> Shall I see you one day?
> Enveloped in impatience, my soul is bursting
> To the proud remains of the fallen Rome!
> I dream about dales, about fragrant woods,
> About the columns of fallen-down mansions!

Although it is unlikely that Baratynsky had ever read Gogol's bathetic lyric, the rhetoric of this new "Italian" poem, especially such lines as "Shall I see you one day?" mimics Gogol's rhetorical question "Full of expectation, shall I see you?" far more exactly than it does Venevitinov's imperative phrase "My time will come when I manage / To love you with the ecstasy of enjoyment." In 1844, Baratynsky departed for Italy and soon died there. In that same year, he composed two more poems on Italy, "To My Italian Tutor" ("Diad'ke-Italiantsu") and "The Steamer" ("Piroskaf"). In them, we find the same "golden lemon" ("limon zlatoi") and "earthly Elysium" ("Eliziii zemnoi"), that is, Paradise, as in Goethe and Gogol.

The question we might want to ask is, why did Baratynsky exchange his firm Roman step for Romantic clichés, borrowed from Goethe, and already tired in the poems of Venevitinov and Gogol? His first poem, "Rome," is descriptively historical and cannot be taken as an expression of some heartfelt need for the real Italy, but the second openly states his personal aspiration to go there. The wish to escape from northern Russia to warm Italy is utterly human and reasonable, of course, and it fits with the equally hackneyed Romantic opposition of North to South that we find in Lermontov and Tiutchev as well as in Pushkin even earlier. Still, why must this natural human longing be immediately plugged into a lexicon that is so trivial?

In fact, the human desire to be in Italy was *unavoidably* Romantic. This, figuratively speaking, Siamese longing evidently knew no other language in which to express itself but the one characterized by a sweetened vocabulary based on the accentuated and exaggerated comparison of the southern characteristics of Italy with stereotypes of the north. If "our" northern sky is gloomy, then the Italian is blue; if the northern sun is stingy, then the Italian is bright, and so on. For the Romantic mind of any caliber, Rome is lost a priori, and it must be regained either through language or through the physical effort of actually going there or, preferably, both.

It is noteworthy that the only thing that actually *differentiates* all three Russian poems from Goethe's "Mignon" is their persistent emphasis on the *soul* as the driving force of the longing to escape to Italy. In Gogol, the soul "pines" for Italy and "moans," and it basks in its "rays"; in Venevitinov, we find the belief that not he but his soul "will play freely" there; and Baratynsky's "soul is bursting to the proud remains of fallen Rome." In Goethe, by contrast, the "dahin"-gesture is distinctly bodily and no soul is even mentioned.

One more thing that connects the Russian poems is the role Italy plays in them as some father- or motherland. In Venevitinov, Italy is the "fatherland of inspiration"; in Baratynsky of both 1821 and 1843, it is "the motherland of man" and the "motherland of voluptuousness," respectively. At first glance, Gogol's loosely Romantic poem appears to avoid this cliché. However, the fact that "Italy" was published in *Son of the Fatherland* (*Syn*

Otechestva) could not have been unmarked by Gogol's oversensitive ear. Most probably, exactly for him this coincidence sounded like the voice of destiny. While Venevitinov died without seeing Italy and Baratynsky died having just arrived, Gogol left for the real Italy some eighteen years after his poem was published and managed to stay there almost until the end of his life.

ROME REGAINED

The concepts of the "soul" and "motherland" as applied to Italy are intriguing. Having found himself in Rome in 1837—and this was already his second visit to the great city—Nikolai Vasilievich Gogol wrote to Vasilii Andreevich Zhukovsky as openly as any son of Vasilii could have written to his own father:

> If you just imagined with what a great pleasure I left Switzerland and flew to my sweetheart, to my beautiful Italy! She is mine! Nobody in the whole world will take her from me. I was born here. Russia, Petersburg, snow, scoundrels, department, university, theater,—I have just dreamed it all. Once more, I woke up in my motherland. . . .[6]

Gogol's decision has been made: Italy *is* his motherland. But where has Ukraine, Gogol's real and worshipped motherland, gone? Did it blend into Italy? Or were they, perhaps, identical twins? Does that not sound a little bit too "Gogolian"? As a matter of fact, Gogol was not the first Ukrainian to equate the two countries. The first displacement of this kind was performed by Ivan Kotliarevsky in his "after Virgil" but nevertheless original version of *The Aeneid* of 1798. There, the Romans wear the wide red trousers of Ukrainian Cossacks and speak with a Poltava accent; in the American case, the effect is as if the antique heroes were dressed up like cowboys and spoke in southern accents. Kotliarevsky's epic starts:

> Еней був парубок моторний
> І хлопець хоч куди козак,
> Удавсь на всеє зле проворний,
> Завзятійший од всіх бурлак.
> Но греки, як спаливши Трою,
> Зробили з неї скирту гною,
> Він, взявши торбу, тягу дав;
> Забравши деяких троянців,
> Осмалених, як гиря, ланців,
> П'ятами з Трої накивав.[7]

> Aeneas was an animated guy
> and a first-rate Cossack.
> He played the agile one in all that's evil,
> a beefy redneck, tougher than the others.
> But when the Greeks, having burned down Troy,
> made it a pile of shit,
> he, having taken his sack, moved his ass out;
> picked up some Trojans,
> all smoked, ragged guys, like weights,
> and nodded his heels to Troy.

Kotliarevsky's travesty is an impressive piece of late eighteenth-century ornate poetry, but Gogol's approach to the Ukraine/Italy displacement was different from his compatriot's. First, when speaking about Italy, Gogol stays away from the mockery or parody we might expect from him and that we easily observe in Kotliarevsky; second, he does not sound acerbic, although sarcasm is what we would normally expect from Gogol. The whole tone of his rhetoric, when the real Italy is his subject, is quite elevated, which in Gogol's case means that he is *very* serious. This same elevated and unalloyed tone had appeared only few times before in his work—in the famous description of the mighty river Dnieper in "A Horrible Revenge" from the collection *Evenings on a Farm near Dikanka* of 1831 to 1832 and in the epic "Taras Bulba" of 1833 to 1835. Both the collection and the epic were devoted to Ukraine. Third, when calling Italy his motherland, Gogol has some more abstract concepts in mind.

In another letter from Rome (this time it was sent to a lady, and women addressees usually drew out Gogol's "philosophical" side), he writes:

> When I finally saw Rome for the second time, oh, it appeared to be even more beautiful than before! It was as if I saw my motherland in which I had not been for a few years,—only my thoughts lived there. No, it is not right: not my motherland, but my *soul's motherland* I saw, the one, where my soul had lived before me, before I was born [emphasis added].[8]

Gogol-the-person seems to be humanly frank here: he feels good and has come back to a paradise-like land. No wonder. Italy is gorgeous enough to evoke such emotion, especially when one sees it closely and not just in Romantic dreams. However, to this common sentiment must be added another, less ordinary, appearance: that of Gogol-the-metaphysician. For *this* Gogol, Italy is not just a gorgeous country but, significantly, his "soul's motherland."

Why is this detail so important? We remember that in his early poem Gogol has already named Italy the land where his soul resides, an obvious tribute to the Romantic tradition. At the same time, in the same poem he avoided labeling Italy a father- or motherland. Now, sixteen years later, he not only repeats his poem's declaration that his "thoughts speak" about Italy—"only my thoughts lived there"—but he calls Italy his soul's motherland, which in epistolary prose looks much more poetic than would have been the case in poetry.

In fact, Gogol's statement on his soul's location is both an attempt to catch up with other Romantics and an expression of his belief in what was behind the common Romantic argot. The concept of the soul's motherland almost immediately leads us to the Platonists, from whom one learns that our soul-Psyche was once expelled from Eden and has been trying, ever since, to find its "paradise lost." The Russian Romantics favored Plato in particular. His world of the ideas galvanized the ghostly lyrics of Vasilii Zhukovsky as well as the German-by-preference muse of Dmitry Venevitinov. The latter even wrote a poetic treatise, "A Conversation between Plato and Anaxagoras," and reported to a friend: "I read him [Plato] almost without difficulty and cannot stop wondering at him, thinking about him."[9] What is more, Gogol was interested, too. The Platonic background of Gogol's works has been discussed in detail many times, most recently by Mikhail Weiskopf.[10] Our writer's interest in the Platonists, for whom the concept of the soul was paramount, becomes evident from Gogol's notes for his lectures on world history at St. Petersburg University. In them, we find a piece on the Platonists written between 1833 and 1834:

> Ammonius—Saccas. [The teacher of Plotinus; the latter stayed with him for eleven years.] Because Christianity resembles Plato and Aristotle, it is the truth; the rest was added by his students. Believed in the variety of unseen spirits, who are seen only by the soul. . . . Plotinus was under the patronage of the Emperor Gallienus, who intended to rebuild for him a provincial city with all its suburbs and villages and to colonize them with philosophers in order to make Plato's republic possible. . . . [Plotinus] said that all that is divine in his soul wants to unify with the divine soul. His treatise, that souls are not two but one, that imagined objects are not outside the mind.[11]

The last phrase, that "imagined objects are not outside the mind," works as a footnote to the epistolary admission about "thoughts" that had "lived" in Italy before he arrived as well as to the line from Gogol's early poem about his "thoughts" "speaking" about Italy. What is more, in order to make Gogol's phrase even clearer, one has to recall briefly one of Plotinus's major points. According to it, νοῦς, the supreme mind, is that essence where our thoughts and objects of our thoughts unite. Italy, so to speak, becomes Gogol's earthly *nus,* analogous to "the nose" linguistically.[12]

The epistolary excerpts from Gogol indicate that Italy managed to cover two central spots on the Gogolian map: his actual motherland and his platonic country. The question of the superimposition of two countries on one brings Plato up again, this time directly. In Plato's *Symposium* (189 e-191 e), we are introduced to an Orphic legend about the androgynous beings (among other complete beings) whom Zeus punished for their pride, cutting them lengthwise and turning their faces as well as their genitals to the cut sides. Since then, according to Plato, humans have been looking for their other halves, and when two halves find each other "eros" occurs.[13] The Gogol who calls Italy his "sweetheart," his "beautiful Italy," whom "nobody in the whole world will take" from him, and so forth, sounds intensely erotic, a state that was highly unusual for the writer. Ukraine, with its "voluptuous nights" ("Taras Bulba"), and "beautiful Italy" seem to be compatible in Gogol's perception with himself, so as to offer completion into a platonic androgynous being. Both Italy and Ukraine (Little Russia) are feminine nouns in Russian (*Italiia,* and *Ukraina* or *Malorossiia*). Italy's feminine gender in Russian explains why, in the second poem of Baratynsky and in Gogol's letters, it is called *rodina,* that is, the motherland.

But both of these can also be seen as male counterparts. For obvious reasons, Rome (in Russian called by the masculine noun *Rim*) metonymically represents the whole of Italy. This is why, both in the first poem on Rome by Baratynsky and in Venevitinov's, we see a characteristic displacement: Venevitinov calls Italy not the motherland but the fatherland *(otchizna),* and Baratynsky calls Rome the motherland *(rodina)* instead of the fatherland. In the case of Kiev (the present-day capital of Ukraine), which is grammatically masculine and also represents the whole of Russia, this same displacement exists: Kiev is traditionally called "the mother of Russian cities" and not the father. In the Russian tradition this formula for Kiev is as ancient as Kiev itself and cannot be modified. What is more, Russia, a feminine noun, can be either the motherland or the fatherland.

For Gogol both countries finally met in 1837, although he had probably felt himself a son of both already from the time his "Italy" had been published in *Son of the Fatherland.* The fact that Gogol decided to stay and reside in Italy seemed to his contemporaries as either a kind of escape or a fresh eccentricity. Were I unjust, I would say that they had not read Gogol carefully enough. For Gogol's adoption of Rome in 1837 had been prognosticated as early as 1829, the year of his first publication. And even if his friends did not know about the existence of his minor poem, Gogol had reaffirmed his point in 1835, the year his collection *Mirgorod* was published.[14] In it, as I will show, Gogol's soul (a feminine noun in Russian), "thematically" expelled to Ukraine, seems to be striving to regain its own lost Rome, so to speak, in order to acknowledge its androgynous unity. It is that seemingly inescapable pull to Rome through Ukraine that illustrates Gogol-the-fatalist best.

APPROACH TO THE BOOK 1: *MIRGOROD* AND MIRGOROD: URBANUS ET VERBUM

Mirgorod provokes questions right from its title, which is unquestionably a weird one. Why is the entire collection called *Mirgorod,* when the actual Mirgorod, a small city near Poltava, is mentioned as a city and a place of narration only in the last (albeit first-written story) of the collection: "The Tale of How Ivan Ivanovich Quarreled with Ivan Nikiforovich"? In addition to its cameo appearance in this one story, Mirgorod emerges only in the two short epigraphs, attributed to others but written by Gogol himself, that precede the collection. "Mirgorod," Gogol writes in the first, "is a voluntarily not big city on the river Khorol. It has 1 rope-yard, 1 brickworks, 4 water- and 45 windmills. *From Ziablovsky's Geography.*" In the second he tells us: "Though the bagels in Mirgorod are baked from rye dough, they are quite tasty. *From The Notes of One Traveler.*"

The question remains, why was *Mirgorod* chosen by Gogol to be the title for the whole book? And, as a corollary, why were not such stories as "The Portrait" and "Nevsky Prospect" included in this collection, even though they were written at more or less the same time? This puzzling issue was raised by Grigory Gukovsky in his book *The Realism of Gogol.* Gukovsky writes:

> One could say that the "Petersburg" tales were not included in *Mirgorod* because they are about Petersburg, and only tales with a Ukrainian theme found their place in *Mirgorod.* This explanation would be incorrect for two reasons. First of all, it already admits, although somehow superficially, the presence in *Mirgorod* of some inner integrity. Secondly, it assumes some predetermination of the title *Mirgorod* (by the way, it sounded weird and not quite clear even to the writer's contemporaries) and the Ukrainian theme. Could Gogol not have called his collection something else? Could he not have put into the first part of his collection all the "Ukrainian" tales and all the "Petersburg" tales into a second? Had he not been bound here by the inner idea content of the collection, would he not have been the boss, free to find dozens of different ways to organize the external composition of his book?[15]

Although Gukovsky did not even try to decipher this weird title, his hunch that there must be a certain connection between it and the entire idea of *Mirgorod* sounds absolutely right to me. Otherwise, why *Mirgorod?*

In order to solve this puzzle one probably should presume that Mirgorod is not only a *name* of some hopelessly small Ukrainian city but also a *word*—and what is more, a meaningful one, as are almost all names in

Gogol. It consists of two parts—*mir* and *gorod*. In Russian and in Ukrainian, *mir* means either "peace" or "world."[16] *Gorod* means a city. Consequently, we get two word pairs: "world-city" and "peace-city."[17] For Gogol's mind, as we will see, *mirgorod* turns out to be an androgynous body.

"World-city" presents a detectable correlation with the Latin expression *urbi et orbi* (a masculine-feminine pair translated as "to Rome and to the world"), a fact that somehow appears to have escaped anyone's notice up to now. With these words the pope usually addressed himself to the Catholic world. As an expression, *urbi et orbi* was widely used by Russians. Thus, for example, Aleksandr Herzen writes in his memoirs about Gogol's famous contemporary Petr Chaadaev, who converted to Catholicism: "The strict order and proud independence of the Western Church, its irreversible confidence and imaginary removal of all controversies by its supreme unity, its immortal fata morgana, its *urbi et orbi*, its disdain of any temporal power, must easily have taken over the fervid mind." (*My Past and Thoughts*, XXX) Anticipating a bit, one might say that this description fits Gogol's approach to Rome as well.

It is no wonder why exactly the *urbi et orbi* wording magnetized Catholics. *Urbi* and *orbi*, two words that differ by only one vowel, form an ideological pun, which—even linguistically—insists on Rome's equivalence to the entire world. But what is also intriguing, *Rim* (Rome) and *mir* (world) are frequently used palindromes in Russian, and this bit of wordplay indicates, no less conclusively than in Latin, that these two are actually one.[18] Unquestionably then, exactly the word *Mirgorod* would be the best possible translation in Russian for *urbi et orbi*, that is, for what Rome is for the cultural, political, and linguistic insight of the Latin tongue.[19] Mirgorod-the-city works very well as an umbrella for Rome-the-concept.

APPROACH TO THE BOOK 2: WAR AND PEACE

What about the second word pair, "peace-city," then?

At first sight, it seems to be an unreliable label for a book whose major topic is not peace but war. Already in the first story, "Old-World Landowners," we find a "war" with food and boredom. The heroes, Afanasy Ivanovich and Pulkheria Ivanovna, consume food instead of events; their simple lives are empty while their stomachs are full of complex meals. In the second story, the epic "Taras Bulba," we see an actual war of Cossacks against Poles. The third, "Viy," describes a fatal war with evil spirits. And the fourth, "The Tale of How Ivan Ivanovich Quarreled with Ivan Nikiforovich," is a "war" between two men. Where is the "peace" then?

In the first and fourth stories, however, my scare quotes around war are not for nothing. Already Andrei Bely in *The Craft of Gogol* pointed out that in *Mirgorod* the first and fourth tales are either a parodic foreshadowing or a sequel to the second and third tales. He gives numerous examples to which I will add just a few.

In fact, the Homeric epic, which Gogol tried to match in his "Taras Bulba," finds its mild parody in "Old-World Landowners." There, the initially Homeric and exhaustibly extended "catalogue of ships," which Osip Mandelstam will try in the twentieth century as a cure for his insomnia, is mockingly replaced by Gogol with a kind of catalogue of . . . food.

"What would you like to have now, Afanasy Ivanovich? Would you like biscuits with lard or poppy-seed pies, or perhaps salted mushrooms?"

"Perhaps mushrooms or pies," answered Afanasy Ivanovich; and the table would at once be laid with a cloth, pies, and mushrooms.

An hour before dinner Afanasy Ivanovich would have another snack, would empty an old-fashioned silver goblet of vodka, would eat mushrooms, various sorts of dried fish, and so on. They sat down to dinner at twelve o'clock. Besides the dishes and sauce bowl there stood on the table numbers of pots with closely covered lids so that no appetizing masterpiece of old-fashioned cookery might be spoiled. At dinner the conversation usually turned on subjects closely related to the dinner. "I think this porridge," Afanasy Ivanovich would say, "is a little bit burned. Don't you think so, Pulkheria Ivanovna?" "No, Afanasy Ivanovich. You put a little more butter in it, then it won't taste burned, or have some more of this mushroom sauce; pour that over it!" "Perhaps," said Afanasy Ivanovich, passing his plate. "Let us try how it would be.". . .

"What would you like?" Pulkheria Ivanovna would say. "Shall I go and tell them to bring you the fruit dumpling I ordered them to keep especially for you?"

"That would be nice," Afanasy Ivanovich would answer.

"Or perhaps you would like some jelly?"

"That would be good too," Afanasy Ivanovich would answer. Then all this was promptly brought him and duly eaten.

Before supper Afanasy Ivanovich would have another snack or something. At half past nine they sat down to supper.[20]

Gogol knows that the Homeric catalogue must be long; however, he does not forget for a moment that the adjective "homeric" in Russian usually goes together with "laughter" *(gomericheskii smekh),* and thus he makes his catalogue hilarious, that is, parodic.

As for "The Tale of How Ivan Ivanovich Quarreled with Ivan Nikiforovich," it unambiguously echoes "Viy," which precedes it. In "Viy," the scared protagonist Thomas Brutus, while reading prayers over the dead witch, draws a circle around himself in order to protect his life from her attacks. In "The Tale . . . ," this situation is reversed when Ivan Ivanovich, having crossed his border with Ivan Nikiforovich (the "border" in "The Tale . . ." functions as an analogue to "Viy's" "circle," because it is supposed to protect Ivan Ivanovich from his hated neighbor), becomes scared:

> His eyes were burning and he could see nothing because of terror. All at once he uttered a cry and almost fainted; he thought he saw a corpse [here we go!], but soon he recovered on perceiving that it was the goose [in the goose he sees himself, because Ivan Nikiforovich's curse "gander" was the cause of the "war" between two Ivans] craning its neck at him.[21]

Gogol's self-parodic hints in "The Tale . . ." at "Taras Bulba" are as transparent as they are at "Viy." There, for example, the gun is what shoots and kills Andrii (who has betrayed the Ukrainians for a Polish beauty), after a brief Homeric duel with his own father, Taras[22]: "Stand still, stir not! I begot you, and now I shall kill you!" said Taras, and stepping back he took the gun from his shoulder."[23] In "The Tale . . . ," the gun is what does *not* shoot but revives the plot and initiates the amusing war between two Ivans: "You go on about your gun, Ivan Nikiforovich, like a crazy child with a new toy," said Ivan Ivanovich with annoyance, for he was really beginning to feel angry. "And you, Ivan Ivanovich, are a regular gander."[24]

The examples of lowering in *Mirgorod* are inexhaustible. Indeed, it seems that the cross-pieces connecting the tales are built from distorting mirrors that reflect all four simultaneously. War in "Old-World Landowners" and in "The Tale of How Ivan Ivanovich Quarreled with Ivan Nikiforovich" is portrayed more as "war in peace," with a major stress on "peace." And that is why, I think, "peace-city" is passable as an extra key to the *Mirgorod* title, too. But how does this key fit Gogol's Italian topic?

APPROACH TO THE BOOK 3: BEAUTY AND THE PEACE

In his essay of 1832 published in *Arabesques,* "A Glance at the Composition of Little Russia," Gogol writes about the genesis of Ukraine:

> With the passing of the first terror [of the Tatars], the expatriots from Poland, Lithuania and Russia gradually began to settle this land [the future Ukraine], the real homeland of the Slavs, the land of the ancient plainsmen and Northerners, the pure Slavonic tribes which in Great Russia were already beginning

to crossbreed with the Finns, but here they were preserved in their former virginal state with all their primitive beliefs, childish prejudices, songs, tales and Slavonic mythology which was confused with Christianity in such a simple-minded way.... Despite the mixed character of the population, there were none of those internecine wars here which had not yet ceased in the heart of Russia: the danger surrounding them on all sides did not allow them. And Kiev—the ancient mother city of Russia—so violently destroyed by the fearsome horse owners, remained poor for a long time and could scarcely compare with the numerous, relatively insignificant towns of Northern Russia. Everyone abandoned it, even the scribe-monks for whom it had always been sacred. Information about it suddenly ceased, and despite the fact that a scion of the Russian princes remained there, nothing could save it from half a century of oblivion. Only occasionally, as if in a dream, the scribes tell us that it suffered terrible destruction and that the Khans' tax gatherers were there—then it was hidden from them as if by some impenetrable curtain.[25]

Gogol's conception of Ukraine as a kind of sleeping beauty who was separated (and preserved!) from the outer world "as if by some impenetrable curtain" is quite original. But what is more surprising, his concept of Rome almost duplicates it exactly. If in this essay Gogol contrasts sleepy, peaceful Ukraine with historically turbulent Russia, then in the fragment "Rome," published in 1842, he sets off Rome against snarled Paris, that is, Italy against France. He praises Rome, exactly as Ukraine, for its isolated survival:

Even the spiritual government, this strange preserved spectre from the past, remains here as if to save people from outer influences, so that none of its selfish neighbors would encroach on its individuality, so that its proud character could remain in peace until some specific time. And besides, here in Rome nothing felt dead; in the ruins and in the gorgeous poverty of Rome [compare to the "destroyed" and "poor" Kiev from the essay] were none of the tedious and penetrating feelings from which humans suffer unwillingly when looking at the monuments of a live dying nation. The feeling here was the opposite: it was of clear, solemn peace.[26]

Thus, we may see that the "peaceful" characteristics of both Ukraine and Rome are essential in Gogol's coverage of them. What is more, the Roman milieu in the fragment "Rome" emphatically resembles the whole atmosphere of *Mirgorod,* its bucolic abandonment and peaceful solitude: "He [a young prince, the hero of "Rome"] especially liked the unpretentiousness of the streets—dark, not cleaned up, the absence of yellow and sweet pastel colors on the houses, an idyll within the city: the flock of billy-goats taking their rest in the middle of the pavement, the shouts of children and the invisible presence upon everything of a clear, solemn peace which embraced all men."²⁷

Gogol's concept of beauty, it would seem, is directly related to the state of peace. Ukraine is beautiful because it is peaceful. The same is true of Italy. Moreover, Gogol's characters achieve their most striking beauty in the moment of their final peace, that is, in death. In "Viy," for example, we have the following portrait of the dead witch in the casket: "Never, it seemed, could features have been formed in such striking yet harmonious beauty. She lay as though living." And a bit later: "But there was in her features nothing faded, tarnished, dead; her face was living."²⁸ These phrases almost repeat Gogol's words about Italy from "Rome"—"And besides, here in Rome nothing felt dead; even in the ruins and in the gorgeous poverty of Rome were none of these tedious and penetrating feelings from which humans suffer unwillingly when looking at the monuments of a dying but still living nation."

Simon Karlinsky has pointed out that all beautiful women in Gogol are pale, and, if they are not dead, they look as if they were. From this it may be tempting to conclude, as he does, that Gogol hated women (his male personages, by contrast, are full of life) and was gay. Starting from this information, however, it would be just as easy to guess that Gogol was a necrophiliac or a hermaphrodite. Whatever the "sexual labyrinth" of Gogol may have been, his concept of beauty as shaped by peace is noteworthy, not the least because it has to do with entire countries as well as individuals.

At the same time, we must not forget that it was precisely wars and what Gogol calls "surrounding danger" that made Ukraine and Rome so serene.

DIGRESSION 1: WHAT BOOKS DID PETRUSHKA READ?

> The greatest power the Devil possesses is his capacity to look like something he is not.
> —D. Merezhkovsky, "Gogol and the Devil"²⁹

> I give things their true names, in other words I call Devil "the Devil," I don't deck him out in a magnificent costume à la Byron, because I know that he goes around in an ordinary tailcoat.
> —Gogol's letter to S. T. Aksakov, May 16, 1844³⁰

Battle with the Devil—Gogol reacted strongly to this subject. According to a remark by Vladimir Nabokov, Gogol believed in the existence of the

Devil "far more seriously than he did in that of God."[31] In some cases, in *Dead Souls* for example, this topic is well concealed, and it was of course in Rome that Gogol's novel was finally composed. Sometimes, as in "Viy," it is unmasked, but there the Roman topic is concealed. In "Viy" some personages are coded as evil ones. And their true nature cannot be decoded without the help of their revealed Roman characteristics. Almost the same mechanism works in *Dead Souls:* not Roman, but equally concealed characteristics reveal the evil nature of the novel's characters. The fact that in Gogol's career *Dead Souls* follows *Mirgorod* makes our knowledge of how these hints work essential.

In *Dead Souls,* Chichikov commits the "crime" of purchasing dead serfs. After this scheme has been discovered, the postmaster of the city comes to the conclusion that Chichikov is one Captain Kopeykin. According to the postmaster's story, Kopeykin had no arm and no leg, both having been lost in the war with Napoleon. Eventually, one listener breaks in: "'But excuse me, Ivan Andreyevich,' said the chief of the police, suddenly interrupting him. 'But did you not say yourself that captain Kopeykin had lost both an arm and a leg, while Chichikov . . .'" (chapter 10, p. 221).

As it happens, "The Story of Captain Kopeykin" was the only part of the novel which the Petersburg censorship did not allow to be published in its original form. But Gogol wanted "The Story . . ." to stay in the novel no matter what, and in order to get it through the censorship he changed it entirely. He was even willing to sacrifice some of its satirical piquancy (which many readers of Gogol's manuscript considered to be the story's primary point) to achieve this. Ultimately, Gogol's willingness to revise and his insistence on the inclusion of this flowery story should suggest that it contains something far more important than satire.

Iurii Mann has claimed that the story's goal is merely patriotic: that in Captain Kopeykin Gogol portrayed national carelessness and boldness and that he derived Kopeykin's name from the proverb "life is a kopeck" (*zhizn'-kopeika*).[32] Mann also suggests that Gogol inherited his captain, together with his lost leg, from a folk song about the thief Kopeykin in the Kireevsky collection. There, a certain Kopeykin narrates a bad dream to his gang:

"Нехорош-то мне, братцы, сон приснился:
Будто я, добрый молодец, хожу по край морю,
Я правою ногою оступился,
За крепкое деревце ухватился,
За крепкое дерево, за крушину.
Не ты ли меня, крушинушка, сокрушила:
сушит да крушит добра молодца печаль-горе!
Вы кидайтеся-бросайтеся, братцы, в легки лодки,

Гребите, ребятушки, не робейте,
Под те ли же под горы, под Змеины!"
Не лютая тут змеюшка прошипела,
Свинцовая тут пулюшка пролетела.³³

"A very bad dream, my friends, I have had:
As if I, a stout fellow, was walking along the sea-shore;
My right leg tripped,
A fragile tree I caught,
A fragile tree, a buckthorn.
It was not you, o buckthorn, that destroyed me:
Sorrow-grief has dried out and afflicted the stout fellow!
Go, my friends, jump into the light boats,
Row, my children, don't be afraid,
Towards the same mountains, the Serpent's!"
It is not a cruel snake that hisses there,
But a lead bullet is flying there.

It is obvious that Gogol was attracted to the song, but what he took from it into his interpolated story, I believe, is not just its patriotic spirit but a characteristic play as well.³⁴ As much as the song plays with words (krushina-the-tree, krushina-the-grief, *krushit'*-to-destroy, *krushit'sia*-to-sorrow) Gogol plays with words' broader meanings. Since "The Story . . ." starts and ends with the absence of Captain Kopeykin's arm and leg, this fact is stressed. But this is only one of the guesses as to who Chichikov might be; in the sequence of different doubles proposed for him, Napoleon's name figures immediately after Kopeykin's. This contrast is of course funny, but there must be something more in it than that.

For many of Gogol's contemporaries, Napoleon in the first place was the equivalent to the Antichrist. He was perceived this way, for example, by Pierre Bezukhov in Leo Tolstoy's *War and Peace*. But what can Kopeykin possibly have in common with the evil Bonaparte when he took part in the war against him? While Napoleon is romantically diabolic, Kopeykin is prosaically so. As one missing an arm and leg, he recalls a serpent, and he behaves like one too, when trying to worm himself into various governmental institutions in order to get paid for his honestly acquired but still devilish feature. (To recall, the thief Kopeykin from the song, like some Saint George, fights the Serpent, too.) Having fought evil, Gogol's Kopeykin, a parody of the song's, becomes a part of it. In the open ending of "The Story . . ." Kopeykin turns into a "robber chief of the Riazan forest"—another parodic Gogolian deflation of the heroic, Robin Hood-like Kopeykin from the song.

What Kopeykin demonstrates, then, is that in *Dead Souls* good and evil are not so much opposed to each other as they are two sides of a very thin coin, that is, still another androgynous pair.

We somehow feel pity for Kopeykin because he is a petty devil (even his name is Mr. Penny—for in English, "penny" would be an alternative for the Russian kopeck—*kopeika*). Vladimir Nabokov, who called Chichikov a "traveling salesman from Hades"; Dmitry Merezhkovsky, who was even more unambiguous on Chichikov ("Chichikov is the Antichrist"); and the officials of the city NN who compare him to Kopeykin and Napoleon all ultimately agree on this personage's devilish nature. In addition to Kopeykin's serpentlike characteristics, the fact that his nature was also meant by Gogol as devilish can be seen through the coincidence that only *demonic* personages are connected to the novel's nationalistic idea: Chichikov travels in a "bird-troika," and it is Kopeykin who fights Napoleon. Typically Russian, Gogol's is a patriotism with bitterness.

In the context of the fact that those in Gogol who deal with evil are devilish themselves (albeit without realizing it), it is noteworthy that Chichikov's servant, Petrushka, is the spit and image of Kopeykin. He is not a worm, but a bookworm, who reads everything he gets his hands on. Much like Kopeykin, he reflects Chichikov. The master and the servant are both infected by the evil, though in different dosages. Paraphrasing the proverb, one might say that the apple handed to Eve by Satan does not fall far from the apple tree.

When Petrushka, this other pitiful petty devil, reads books, he totally neglects their contents:

> By nature he was reserved rather than loquacious; he even had a noble urge for enlightenment, that is, for reading books without paying much heed to their content. It was a matter of absolute indifference to him whether he was reading about the adventures of an infatuated hero, a simple primer, or a prayer-book: he perused all these books with equal attention; if a treatise on chemistry had been slipped in front of him, he would not have disdained it. What pleased him was not so much what he read as just reading or, rather, the process of reading, the fact that letters were always composing some sort of word, which sometimes meant the devil only knows what.[35]

Why does Petrushka not see the content behind the words? Why do they mean "the devil only knows what"? Unlike Gogol, he simply does not recognize that there is nothing in the content that is not already in the word. Let us not forget, however, that even though Petrushka did not care what he read, his reading list consisted of heroic life histories and of prayers.

RETURN TO THE PLOT 1: NAMES AS THE ULTIMATE KEY WORDS

> Public tragedies give dressy names to
> naked places.
> —A. Gopnik[36]

"Viy" is probably Gogol's least analyzed work. On the surface, it is such a Halloween story that the only question scholars usually worry about is why Viy is called Viy. Gogol, in his footnote, says that this "is the name among Little Russians for the chief of the gnomes," a mystification (no such creature exists in folklore) that precedes those of J. L. Borges by more than a century. There is, of course, nothing wrong with enjoying "Viy" as a horror story, which it is, too. In so doing, however, we inevitably repeat Petrushka's way of reading: the "devil only knows" what the story means.

The story's plot is intriguing. During his vacation, the Ukrainian seminarist—philosopher, as Gogol calls him—Thomas Brutus, along with two friends, is caught by night at the godforsaken farmstead of an ugly old woman. In the middle of the night, this woman visits Thomas, jumps on his back, and starts riding him as if he were a horse through neighboring fields and forests. Thomas contrives to slip out from under the woman, and this time he gets her saddled. Beaten by Thomas, the old woman falls to the ground and turns into a dying young beauty. Thomas runs away and returns to the seminary. Soon after, he is summoned to the rector in order to be sent to one of the richest Cossack captains to read prayers over his late daughter for three nights. It is said that Thomas had been her own choice before she died. Thomas arrives at the Captain's estate, sees the beautiful daughter in the coffin, and recognizes in her the witch he had beaten to death. During the first night in the church where the witch's coffin has been placed, she arises in order to destroy Thomas, but he draws a circle around himself and the witch cannot pass through it. Having turned gray after a second night marked by intensified horrors, Thomas wants to escape but does not manage. On the third night, a huge collection of morbid evil spirits enters the church and with them they bring Viy, at whom Thomas is not supposed to look. He cannot help himself, however, and as soon as he sees Viy, he dies. The evil spirits are nevertheless caught in the church by sunrise and they die, too. The church is never revisited afterward. Thomas's two friends, who had been with him at the witch's farmstead at the beginning of the story, get together and mourn over him on the final page. "Viy" is indeed uncanny. At the same time, the story's frolicsome pitch makes it less horrific than this plot summary would lead one to believe. What does it mean?

Iurii Lotman has pointed out the substantive role of names in Russian eighteenth-century literature. There, names explain everything: Evgeny Negodiaev is a scoundrel (*negodiai* = scoundrel), Chistiakov is pure and has a tender heart (*chistyi* = clean), Strelinsky is a good officer (*streliat* = to shoot), Nichtovich is a skeptic (*nichto* = nothing). As a child, Gogol took part in many amateur performances of eighteenth-century theatrical work, and the importance of names was well known to him. As a writer, he follows the same track. Gogol's names are talking, though it takes a bit of work to make them say anything distinct.

At the very beginning, we meet three friends: the theologian Khaliava, the philosopher Thomas Brutus, and the rhetorician Tiberius Gorobets (his last name is derived from the Ukrainian word for "sparrow"). All three bear such aggressively unique names that this fact alone ought to make us suspect that they signify something. In particular, two of them—Brutus and Tiberius—are taken directly from Roman history. This fact, remarkably, has been overlooked by all English translators, who for some reason render the names as they sound in Russian—that is Khoma Brut and Tibery Gorobets—instead of translating them.

While Thomas Brutus's Roman part, Brutus, serves as his last name, the Roman emperor provides the first name of Tiberius Gorobets. The other parts of both names are Ukrainian. I will wait to unfold the meaning of Khaliava, the third name of the trio, because it plays the role of the ultimate key to Gogol's code in "Viy."

In his famous essay "How 'The Overcoat' is Made," after analyzing the way Gogol employs names, Boris Eichenbaum points out that the story combines verbal play "with a highly emotional, declamatory style which forms . . . a secondary layer."[37] Although both of the grand Roman names in "Viy" are similarly lowered by their juxtaposition with common Ukrainian names, they are far too famous in Roman history to be left out as unimportant. Because of them, the secondary layer of the story, though it officially takes place in Ukraine, is apparently mapped out as Roman. It remains to be seen, however, what this knowledge contributes to our reading.

APPROACH TO THE PLOT 1: TWO BRUTUSES AND THE UNKNOWN PARENT

> *Socrates:* Now notice what, starting from this state of perplexity, he will discover by seeking the truth in company with me, though I simply ask him questions without teaching him. . . . This knowledge will not come from

> teaching but from questioning. He will recover it for himself.
>
> *Meno:* Yes.
>
> *Socrates:* And the spontaneous recovery of knowledge that is in him is recollection, isn't it?
>
> *Meno:* Yes.
>
> —Plato, *Meno*[38]

Thomas Brutus, who bears the heaviest burden of the events in "Viy," deserves to be dealt with first. He, of course, shares his name with Marcus Junius Brutus (85?-42 B.C.), one of Caesar's assassins. In its juxtaposition to "Thomas," "Brutus" somehow shrinks in its Roman glory, and together the two create a somewhat comic effect. For this reason, it would be simplistic to think that Gogol has merely provided a Ukrainian adaptation of Marcus Junius Brutus's biography.

The murder of Caesar, of course, is the key point in Marcus Junius Brutus's life. The murder of the witch marks the same key point in the life of our hero. From this point on, both lives, previously quite placid, follow a death vector, which leads Thomas to the lost combat with evil in the church, and Marcus Junius—fighting the army of Mark Antony and Octavian, later the Emperor Augustus—to the lost battle at Philippi. What is more, both Brutuses are almost victorious but lose their battles at the very last moment, when their death vector overpowers apparent victory. Thomas Brutus, unbeaten for two nights, nevertheless dies on the third. Marcus Junius, who defeated Octavian in the first engagement of the battle at Philippi, was nevertheless crushed in his second encounter. In despair, Brutus committed suicide.

In addition to being a murderer of Caesar and a warrior for the Republic, Marcus Junius Brutus is famed for being, allegedly, Caesar's illegitimate son. Rumors on this score were common. According to Plutarch's biography of Brutus in his *Parallel Lives*. . . .

> It is said that Caesar had so great a regard for him [Brutus] that he ordered his commanders by no means to kill Brutus [who was in the army of Caesar's enemy, Pompey] in the battle, but to spare him if possible, and bring him safe to him, if he would willingly surrender himself; but if he made any resistance, to suffer him to escape rather than do him any violence. And this he is believed to have done out of a tenderness to Servilia, the mother of Brutus; for Caesar had, it seems, in his youth been very intimate with her, and she passionately in love with him; and, considering that Brutus was born about that time in which their loves were at the highest, Caesar had a belief that he was his own child.[39]

Moreover, according to the Roman historian Suetonius, Caesar avowed the relationship just before he died:

> Confronted by a ring of drawn daggers, he [Caesar] drew the top of his gown over his face, and at the same time ungirded the lower part, letting it fall to his feet so that he would die with both legs decently covered. Twenty-three dagger thrusts went home as he stood there. Caesar did not utter a sound after Casca's blow had drawn a groan from him; though some say that when he saw Marcus Brutus about to deliver the second blow, he reproached him in Greek with: "You, too, my child?"[40]

The fact that Brutus, who had grown up in a hazy atmosphere of rumors that Caesar was his real father, got sudden confirmation directly from Caesar and just at the instant before the latter died makes his image almost similar to Sophocles's Oedipus, who killed his father, Laius. Once inside the Greek paradigm of parent slayers, we should also perhaps keep in mind a possible connection to Aeschylus's Orestes, the murderer of his mother, Clytemnestra. Given what we have already seen of Gogol's tendency to juggle male and female roles, at least linguistically, the connection of patricide and matricide is not far-fetched. But does Thomas Brutus fit the same pattern? In order to find out, one has to investigate Thomas's connection with the witch.

Their first encounter takes place at the witch's farmstead. She rides Thomas, and then he rides her, while beating her with a piece of wood. Having beaten the witch to death, Thomas faces a young beauty instead of the ugly old witch:

> He stood up and looked into her eyes: there was the glow of sunrise, and the golden domes of the Kiev churches were gleaming in the distance. Before him lay a beautiful girl with luxuriant tresses all in disorder and eyelashes as long as arrows. Senseless, she tossed her bare white arms and moaned, looking upward with eyes full of tears. Thomas trembled like a leaf on a tree; he was overcome by pity, strange emotion and timidity, feelings he could not himself explain. He began running, full speed. His heart throbbed uneasily as he went, and he could not account for the strange new feeling that had taken possession of it.[41]

The peculiar thing about this fragment is that Thomas does not feel the emotions we would expect from someone who has undergone such a traumatic experience. There is no mention, for example, of horror (although his trembling might lead us to believe he has experienced it) or, even more important, relief or repentance. Instead we are told of a "strange new feel-

Writing as Exorcism

ing" of "pity, strange emotion and timidity," as if in this situation he has been stimulated to begin to discover something new to him. At the same time, in the witch's eyes, as in some fairy-tale crystal ball, he sees his own future (although he does not recognize this at the time): a church and sunrise, or the "third watch," at which he will die at the end of the story. What is equally strange is that the witch also has an unusual reaction to the situation—her eyes, writes Gogol, are "full of tears." This small detail immediately raises several questions: Is she crying because she regrets dying, or, on the contrary, is she happy to die? Do the tears mean that she recognizes that she should feel remorse for some reason?

The second encounter of Thomas and the witch occurs on the captain's estate, where she lies dead in her coffin. Before Thomas is allowed to see her in it, he is interrogated by the witch's father, the captain:

> "Who are you, where do you come from, and what is your calling, good man?" said the captain, in a voice neither friendly nor ill-humored.
> "A bursar, student in philosophy, Thomas Brutus . . ."
> "Who was your father?"
> "I don't know, honored sir."
> "Your mother?"
> "I don't know my mother either. It is reasonable to suppose, of course, that I had a mother; but who she was and where she came from, and when she lived—I swear, good sir, I don't know."[42]

The captain's first question is already odd. He, who has invited precisely Thomas and personally sent for him at the seminary, now asks about his name, the place he is from, and his profession. And why does he ask Thomas about his parents? It sounds like a job interview, but the captain has no other candidate but Thomas for the "position" of prayer reader because this choice, we soon find out, was his late daughter's.

It is strange enough that Thomas knows nothing about either of his parents. But it is even stranger that when he does speak of them, he talks more about his unknown mother than about his equally unknown father. And why does he do it with such heat, even swearing that he does not know who she was? From this, one gets the feeling that Thomas either does know who his mother is but does not want to reveal it or that he really does not know but is obsessed by the question. That is, he speaks about her all the time to himself and, when asked, just continues aloud his inner monologue. In either case, the issue clearly bothers him.

Finally, the captain asks Thomas whether he knows why his late daughter selected him to read the prayers over her dead body, and Thomas, as expected, does not. The captain then continues:

I should have learned all about it. "Let no else read over me, but send, Father, at once to the Kiev Seminary and fetch the bursar, Thomas Brutus; let him pray three nights for my sinful soul. He knows . . . !" But what he knows, I did not hear: she, poor darling, could say no more before she died.[43]

The situation gets even stranger. The witch's last words, "he knows," and the captain's perplexed phrase, "but what he knows," mix everything up. Indeed, what is it that Thomas knows?

The last words Caesar addressed to Brutus and those that the witch addressed to Thomas Brutus via her father both contain hints leading to unresolvable mysteries. The formula "my child," applied to the historical Brutus by Caesar, is ambiguous. For Brutus can just as well be his spiritual child as his son by blood; Caesar, as we know, was fond of Brutus, taught him, and helped him. Gogol's fictional Brutus, who also appears to have been obsessed with the question of his parentage, receives a nebulous hint that he knows some secret. In both cases, the hints must have worked to increase suspense rather than to clear it up.

In the end, despite some ambiguity, there is enough evidence to consider the Roman Brutus his father's killer; certainly that is the way that history ended up portraying him. Despite the fact that nothing in the story openly tells us what kind of a secret it can be, the only mysterious thing about the Ukrainian double of the supposed Roman patricide remains the utterly strange new feeling he cannot explain even to himself. What he comes to know, eventually (and this knowledge is what kills him in the end), is that he is indeed the double of his Roman namesake, but that he has killed his mother. In so doing, he completes the androgynous pair Caesar/witch and closes the circle Rome/Ukraine. The rest of this analysis will be devoted to showing how he comes to this knowledge.

The initial way to solve this complex problem is through the work of the same philosopher who provided us with the first statement of the androgynous principle: Plato—his concept of the soul, specifically the theory of anamnesis, of knowledge as recollection. In *Meno*, the dialogue in which Plato introduces us to this theory, Socrates tells Meno: "All nature is akin, and the soul has learned everything, so that when a man has recalled a single piece of knowledge—*learned* it, in ordinary language—there is no reason why he should not find out all the rest, if he keeps a stout heart and does not grow weary of the search, for seeking and learning are in fact nothing but recollection."[44]

Given Gogol's Platonism (for which incidents in previous lives were comprehended in what could be recollected) as well as the fantastic context of this story, it is perhaps not surprising that Thomas Brutus knows a secret without having learned it from anybody. This knowledge was already, so to speak, wrapped up in that strange new feeling he got at the beginning of the story. Now in the church, he, with "stout" heart, continues his search and finally achieves full knowledge.

APPROACH TO THE PLOT 2: THE LOST BATTLES AT PHILIPPI AND AT FORTY-SOMETHING MILES FROM KIEV: THE EVIL GENIUS AND VIY

> Несчастный силится напрасно
> Сказать, что нет того, что есть.
> Он правду видит, видит ясно . . .
>
> The wretch tries in vain
> To say that what exists does not.
> He sees the truth, sees it clearly . . .
> —A. Pushkin, "From Ariosto's *Orlando Furioso*"

Orestes, the mother-murderer, and Brutus, the father-killer, both had weighty motives for their crimes: one avenged his father Agamemnon, who had been killed by Orestes's mother and her lover; another stood for the republican cause. Nevertheless, punishment follows both crimes, and what is interesting, it takes the form of a nightmare. Orestes was haunted day and night by the Erinyes, the three ill-looking goddesses of vengeance, and almost lost his mind. On the nightmares of Brutus, Plutarch comments twice, in the biographies of Caesar and of Brutus. In the first, he reports:

> Brutus . . . laid himself down one night, as he used to do, in his tent, and was not asleep, but thinking of his affairs, and what events he might expect. For he is related to have been the least inclined to sleep of all men who have commanded armies, and to have had the greatest natural capacity for continuing awake, and employing himself without need of rest. He thought he heard a noise at the door of his tent, and looking that way, by the light of his lamp, which was almost out, saw a *terrible* figure, like that of a man, but of *unusual stature* and *severe countenance. He was somewhat frightened at first*, but seeing it neither did nor spoke anything to him, *only stood silently by his bedside*, he asked who it was. The spectre answered him, "Thy *evil genius*, Brutus, and thou shalt see me at Philippi." Brutus answered courageously, "Well, I shall see you," and immediately the appearance vanished. When the time was come, he drew up his army near Philippi against Antony and Caesar [later the emperor Augustus], and in the first battle won the day, routed the enemy, and plundered Caesar's camp. The night before the second battle, the

same phantom appeared to him again, but *spoke not a word. He presently understood his destiny was at hand,* and exposed himself to all the danger of the battle. Yet he did not die in the fight, but seeing his men defeated, got up to the top of a rock, and there presenting his sword to his naked breast, and assisted, as they say, by a friend, who helped him to give the thrust, met his death [emphasis added].[45]

In Brutus's biography we find one more interesting detail about his insomnia. According to Plutarch, he "employed himself in *reading until the third watch,* at which time the centurions and tribunes were used to come to him for orders [emphasis added]."[46]

Thomas's insomnia in the story is no less artificial than that of Orestes and almost identical to the way Brutus kept himself awake: he was ordered to read prayers all the night until the third watch, at which time he was free to leave the church. The three nights Thomas spends in the church are shot through not only by horror but also by some strange eye symbolism to which this horror is directly connected.

Night 1

Thomas at first resists the temptation to look at the beautiful witch in her coffin but cannot overpower it. When he finally looks, the face of the witch "was living, and it seemed to the philosopher that she was looking at him with *closed eyes* [emphasis added]."[47] Brutus is frightened that she will rise from the coffin, and she does: "He looked at her widely and *rubbed his eyes.* She was, indeed, not lying down now, but sitting up in the coffin. He *looked away,* and again *turned his eyes with horror on the coffin.* She stood up . . . she was walking about the church with her eyes *shut,* moving her arms back and forth as though trying to *catch* someone [emphasis added]."[48] The frequent mentioning of the eyes or gestures relating to them in this short fragment is puzzling. The witch, who at first was looking at Thomas with closed eyes, now has her eyes shut trying to catch him. Thomas rubs his eyes—a gesture of one who either is trying to wake up or does not believe what he sees. The way Thomas looks and does not look (looks away but turns his eyes to the coffin) parallels the seeing/not seeing eyes of the witch.

Moreover, the eye theme does not stop even after Thomas has drawn a circle around himself and starts reading prayers and pronouncing exorcisms. The witch, writes Gogol, "was coming *straight toward* him. . . . She *stood* almost *on the very line.* . . . Thomas *had not the courage to look at her;* she was terrifying. She ground her teeth and *opened her dead eyes;* but, *seeing nothing,* turned with fury . . . in another direction . . . trying to *catch*

Thomas [emphasis added]." If the witch came straight toward Thomas almost crossing the line, how was it possible that she could not see him? Gogol nevertheless insists she could not. Does this not suggest that the eyes here signify a different kind of sight?

Night 2

Thomas reads the prayers and exorcisms again, but at some point, writes Gogol, "his heart turned *cold;* the corpse was already standing before him on the very edge of the circle, and her *dead, greenish eyes were fixed upon him.*" Thomas, as was the case before, could not resist looking at her, and "with a *sidelong glance out of one eye* he saw that the corpse was feeling for him where he was not standing, and that she evidently could *not* see him."[49] Once again, the situation is the same: the witch approaches Thomas without seeing him, though her eyes are wide open this time. Thomas does not want to look and nevertheless does, while his heart seems to be affected by the corpse's low temperature. It appears that each can see the other as long as they do not attempt to see each other simultaneously. Altogether, we have an exchange of looks while eyes do not really meet: when Thomas looks at the witch, she does not see him even with her eyes fixed on him; on the contrary, when she sees him, her eyes are closed. Does this suggest, as before, that perception is not actually visual here? Does it not recall the situation when Thomas knows something that he cannot possibly know? In "Viy," seeing and simultaneous not seeing matches knowing and not knowing almost exactly.

Years ago, Leon Stilman pointed out that "themes connected with vision, with seeing, occupy an important place in Gogol's writings."[50] Thomas's eyes' gestures are somehow incomplete both nights and, in a manner of speaking, find a middle course (he does not have the courage to look at her; the sidelong glance out of one eye), while the witch at first does look at Thomas even with her eyes shut and finally literally opens them. When her eyes are open, however, she sees something but it is not Thomas. Were we to substitute knowing/not knowing for vision here, it would look as if Thomas is afraid of full knowledge, while the witch "sees" it in full. (The fact that her eyes are "dead" when open might signify that this knowledge is truly dreadful.) Moreover, we recall that Brutus got the very first whiff of a strange new feeling as early as his first encounter with the witch, that is, during their night ride. And the eye symbolism was also present there. What is more, it preceded the new feeling in Brutus's heart: "The forests, the meadows, the sky, the dales, all seemed as though *slumbering with open eyes.* . . . He [Brutus] was aware of an exhausting, unpleasant, and at the same time, voluptuous sensation assailing his heart. . . . *Did he see this or did he not?*"[51]

Here, everything around Brutus seems to be able to "see" a truth he cannot yet see, although he already feels its unpleasant touch. As Plato's Socrates might have said, recollection has probably started.

It is time to recall here the episode with the ghost from the biography of Brutus, for it contains some bizarre parallels to Thomas Brutus's situation in the church. As we remember, the evil genius of Brutus scared him as much as the dead witch scared his Ukrainian counterpart. The apparition appears by Brutus's bedside, while the dead witch stands, also silently, at the very edge of Thomas Brutus's circle, his substitute bed. Presumably Caesar's, the ghost talks to Brutus and brings him bad luck. The witch, on *night two*, starts speaking also, a sort of mumbo-jumbo. Thomas Brutus "heard a hollow mutter, and she [the witch] began pronouncing terrible words with her dead lips. . . . He could not have said what they meant; but there was something fearful in them. The philosopher understood with horror that she was making an incantation."

Although Brutus was concerned the first time the ghost appeared to him, he was nevertheless able to win the initial engagement. Likewise, the witch's incantation, although it brings a "beating of wings on the panes of the church" and "the dull scratching of claws upon iron, and numberless evil creatures thundering on the doors and trying to break in," is survivable. For the time being, Thomas Brutus is saved by the dawn, which makes the evil creatures disappear. In their own ways, then, nights one and two at forty-something miles from Kiev parallel the first, fortunate part of the Philippi battle.

Night 3

At last, the evil creatures bring Viy with them and Brutus loses the battle.

Who is Viy and what does he look like? Gogol indicates that Viy's "long eyelids hung down to the very ground." Moreover, Viy, we find out, is the witch's last engine to force Brutus to see in full. And seeing in full, that is, final knowledge, means in the story that the eyes of both sides must finally meet. And so it happens. "'Lift up my eyelids. I do not see!' said Viy . . . and all the creatures flew to raise his eyelids. 'Do not look!' an inner voice whispered to the philosopher. He could not restrain himself, and he looked. 'There he is!' shouted Viy, and thrust an iron finger at him." Of course, Viy's iron finger means here the so-called finger of fate (in Russian, *perst sud'by*), while Viy's range of vision, to use Leon Stilman's term, is synonymous with fate's all-seeing eye. But what is even more important, Viy's own name links this creature to the final knowledge that Brutus gains and dies for.

As has already been mentioned, the name Viy does not exist in folklore; it is Gogol's invention. Given the fact that names in Gogol are ninety-nine percent meaningful, scholars are amply attuned to the problem of what *viy* means. Speaking ahead, the name Viy is as equally meaningful for the story as is Brutus. Were this not so, Gogol's code would probably escape decoding as successfully as Thomas did from under the old witch. The word *viy* is, I believe, Gogol's personal transformation of the imperative for the verb *videt'* (to see). Instead of its correct form *vizhd'* (see!), which is somehow too solemn and almost biblical, Gogol designs his variant from such imperatives as *stoy* (stand still!) or *voy* (howl! or cry!). It is more than appropriate: Viy-the-creature has a power that recalls Medusa's.[52] "Viy" as the word is an order given to Thomas Brutus: have a good look, and not just a half-look as before! And then, so to speak, cry or die. Brutus could not resist fate's command: though having been warned against doing so by his inner voice, he looked. For the first time, he saw clearly the deadly truth: like Brutus, who killed a tyrant who was his father, our hero murdered the witch who was his mother.

My interpretation of the meaning of the word "Viy" complements the two other most interesting ones that have been proposed—those of Leon Stilman, who suggested that *viy* is derived from the Ukrainian *viya*, meaning "eyelash,"[53] and Simon Karlinsky, who brilliantly tried to prove that it is a modified form of *vuy*, the Ukrainian word for "maternal uncle."[54] Viy, who has "long eyelids," is, of course, a relative of the witch: her eyelashes, Gogol comments twice, are "as long as arrows." Both, the eyelids and the eyelashes, unmistakably stand for shielded vision, and thus, when lifted up, make it clear.

That fact that Viy *is* a blood relative of the witch is significant as well, for the "maternal uncle" personifies the truth about the crime for which Thomas Brutus, as Brutus before him, pays with his own life.

DIGRESSION 2: INSIDE ONE CIRCLE— SERVILIA, MARIIA IVANOVNA, AND THE WITCH

Even if parents are young, they look old to their children.

The witch of "Viy" is at first old but then is young and beautiful.

Servilia, born in 100 B.C., the mother of Marcus Junius Brutus Junior in 85 B.C., was married to Marcus Junius Brutus Senior and remained Gaius Julius Caesar's best-liked mistress for twenty years. Caesar, like Servilia, was born in 100 B.C. If Brutus was Caesar's son, then the age difference between Brutus and his parents was only fifteen years.

Mariia Ivanovna Gogol-Ianovskaia, an oppressive mother to her depressive Nikolai, was also only fifteen or sixteen years older than her son.[55]

There was a legend in Gogol's family, and Mariia Ivanovna loved telling it, about how Vasilii Afanasievich, later Nikolai's father, met her.

Once he had a dream in which the Virgin Mary told him that all his illnesses—Gogol's future father was not a healthy man—would disappear as soon as he was wed. "And here is your wife," said she, according to Mariia Ivanovna, and raised her hand. At Mary's foot Vasilii Afanasievich saw a little girl, whom he could not subsequently forget. The further events were described by Mariia Ivanovna as follows:

> His [Vasilii's] parents, having no church in the neighborhood, used to ride to the small town Iareski on the river Psol. There, he met my aunt, and when the wet-nurse carried out the seven-month-old baby he looked at it and was surprised: in the baby's face, he saw the same features that had appeared in his dream. Not having a word with anybody, he started looking me over; when I was growing up he entertained me with different toys, was not even bored when I played with my dolls . . . , and my aunt never tired of admiring this young man who was not bored to play with such a baby all day long; I knew him very well and, seeing him often, came to love him; then, thirteen years later, he had the identical dream. . . . A girl wearing a white dress and a radiant crown, of indescribable beauty, came out [through the altar doors] and pointing to her left said: "Here is your bride!" He looked and saw a girl in a white dress, who was sitting at her work at small table and had the same face. Soon after we returned from Kharkov, he asked my hand from my parents.[56]

It is noteworthy that the earthly Mary—Mariia is the Russian name for Mary—was sent to Vasilii Gogol also by Mary, the Virgin Mary. The fact that Vasilii managed to see in the baby Mariia the heavenly features from his dream makes him no less a platonist and a fatalist than their future son Nikolai. Did he not see those features in part because the baby was called Mariia? It seems that Nikolai's platonic "paranoia" was inherited even in its linguistic aspect.

Young Mariia Ivanovna truly loved her older husband. After he died in 1825 she nearly starved herself to death. (Nikolai, of course, did die of self-starvation in 1852, a date that "mirrors" 1825.) His father's death found Nikolai already in Nezhin, in a high school *(gymnaziia)*. From there, he immediately wrote to his mother, ostensibly to console her. In the letter, he asked rather rhetorically: "Do I not still have a sensitive, tender and virtuous mother *who will be my father,* my friend, and all that together which is even more dear, even more precious? [emphasis added]"[57] His subsequent visit home provided a scene even more characteristic for his perception of his mother. "Having lost my husband," recalled Mariia Ivanovna, "I was wearing a mourning dress made of the most coarse wool fabric; this made my son really sad: he thought it was too rough and disturbing, though I tried to assure him that I felt no such roughness. When he unexpectedly came home from Nezhin before Christmas break, it was early in the morning. He saw my dress brushed in the ante-room, and ordered scissors to be brought to him in order to cut it to pieces, adding that 'his dear mother will now wear a normal quiet dress.' . . . With what delight did he always come home! Once, observing me from a distance and coming close, he said: 'We are so happy that you are so young and we will stay together for a long time.'"[58]

Gogol clearly had no need of Freud's theory to develop a serious Oedipus complex. He was definitely jealous of his father, and his perception of his mother was certainly erotic. Thomas, taken as a vehicle for a night ride by the witch and having changed places with her, is probably the best illustration of Gogol's sublimated eroticism. It is not for nothing that the feeling Thomas experiences is described as a "fiendishly voluptuous" one *(besovski sladkoe chuvstvo)* and a "stabbing, exhaustingly terrible delight." Thomas does not know that incest has taken place, while Gogol most likely feared and desired it (once an exorcist, Gogol cannot help but exorcising his fears on paper in order to avoid them in the real life.) At the same time, as we have seen from Gogol's letter to his mother, she was also a substitute father (that androgynous pair again!) and thus the matricide of Thomas Brutus, instead of the patricide of the Roman Brutus, is understandable.

DIGRESSION 3: ALL IN THE FAMILY CIRCLE

By drawing a circle around himself, Thomas fences off the truth he is afraid to face. He is, so to speak, shutting himself off from his family. In the moment he finally sees the truth, the shield/circle does not work any more and Thomas dies.

Moreover, another weighty reason to believe that Thomas is indeed the witch's son follows from the contextual logic of *Mirgorod*—the entire collection. In the other three stories, all action is overtly within family circles. To recall, in "Taras Bulba" Andrii, the renegade, is killed by his *own* father Taras and the latter dies in the end of Gogol's epic when avenging another son, Ostap. In the two other stories, "Old-World Landowners" and "The Tale of How Ivan Ivanovich Quarreled with Ivan Nikiforovich," the four heroes—Afanasy Ivanovich and Pulkheria Ivanovna, and Ivan Ivanovich and Ivan Nikiforovich—are all pairs. The first consists of a man and wife (both personages look androgynous!); they even bear the same patronymics—a fact that suggests that they are also brother and sister, and perhaps even foreshadows the incestual relationship in "Viy." As for Ivan Ivanovich and Ivan Nikiforovich, of course, they are merely neighbors, but their love-hate relationships recall family ties more than the polite companionship of neighbors. Moreover, both first names are again identical, or again androgynous, which makes these ties overt linguistically. Consequently, all three stories are about either real families or a unit that substitutes for them. This one fact, I believe, already propels the following question: if three of the four stories of *Mirgorod*'s corpus are *about* family business, why should "Viy," then—the remaining fourth—be different? And if it is different, why was it nevertheless included in Gogol's very well-thought-out collection, while other simultaneously written stories, as has been mentioned before, did not find a place there?

Still, there is one more mystery regarding the relationship of this story to the family unit. Why did Thomas's prayers not protect him? Or, to put it another way, who else was in the family circle that surrounded and ultimately killed the hero? In our discussion of Kopeykin, we already advanced the thesis that in Gogol's world those who fight evil are inevitably evil themselves—a kind of guilt by association; they all belong to one family.[59] This Gogolian society of darkness has many lodges, and no badge that would allow the devils to recognize each other is provided. Thomas, who belongs to the Roman lodge, is a displacement himself: he does not immediately recognize those who belong to the Ukrainian one.

Chichikov, Kopeykin, Petrushka, and Thomas are all orphans. As if wishing to give them a new family, Gogol creates a petty devils' fraternity. But their devilish nature is rather deeply hidden. Tibery Gorobets, Thomas Brutus's friend, belongs to this fraternity, too. He is Tiberius the Sparrow, and thus a cruel Roman tyrant and a bird at once. To recall from the previous chapter, a possible root of Chichikov's name could be the verb *chikat'* (to stab). Another conceivable root, however, would be the sound a Russian sparrow makes: *chik-chirik*.[60] In their names, therefore, both Chichikov and Tiberius contain features of grand/less grand villains and of a small bird, a grayish and not very noticeable one; a bird that is as trivial as a penny-Kopeykin. Petrushka's reading list—prayers and heroic adventures—recalls that of Thomas and, what is more, of Gogol himself. Like Petrushka, Thomas reads prayers, while Gogol was more into heroic biographies: by Plutarch among others.

In addition to the facts of matricide/patricide and of the ghost, Gogol—in one of his usual displacements—gives Thomas that title for which Caesar, on the eve of getting it, was actually killed by Brutus. After his nocturnal adventure, Brutus is taken to the seminary's rector and addressed as "Divine Thomas," an obvious mocking reference to the title of the Roman emperor. Rewritten in "Viy" in a jocular form, Brutus's dramatic life nonetheless retains its meaning. As in "The Nose," the depressive topic is given a comic shape. Moreover, Brutus and Tiberius are not the only Romans in "Viy": the sophomores of the seminary call themselves senators and wear very long garments that resemble Roman togas; thus, they also belong to this secret Roman society of Gogol in *Mirgorod*, its Roman masquerade.

RETURN TO THE PLOT 2: THOMAS'S CRUSADE OF THOMAS

The first names of the Gogolian personages, almost as frequently as their last names, can explain a great deal about their behavior. It is noteworthy that Chichikov's first name is Pavel, that is, Paul, and his patronymic is Ivanovich; that is, his father's name was John (Russian Ivan). Both names are of important saints. It makes Chichikov, figuratively speaking, protected by Saint Paul's dome, his first name, as much as is Thomas in the church. In both cases, however, the church does not help them to escape final punishment.

Thomas's first name is also that of a saint: Saint Thomas. But for Russians and Ukrainians, the names Foma and Khoma are far more exotic than the English Thomas; indeed, they are rarely used in everyday life and instead bring up strong associations with "historical" or "cultural" figures—in particular the biblical Doubting Thomas and Saint Thomas Aquinas. Both of them fit Thomas as a personage. Like the Doubting Thomas, our hero does not believe in facts unless he sees them with his own eyes. But why would exactly Thomas Aquinas be a proper model for Thomas? First, he is as "Italian" as Brutus. Second, he is a philosopher like our hero. Third, he was on Gogol's reading list: from Italy, Gogol asked a friend to send him Aquinas's works.[61] However, the fourth and most important reason for Thomas to bear Aquinas's name is that Saint Thomas was the very first witch hunter. Aquinas, according to Rossell Hope Robbins, denied a formal agreement between man and the Devil, but his concept of a direct contact with Satan became a foundation for future witch hunts. Moreover, Aquinas insisted on the execution of witches, and, according to George Barr, all Satan's abettors and servants came to life from the head of a monastic philosopher.[62]

Thus, even had Gogol's Thomas not been Brutus, he would not have been able to avoid killing the witch. He was, so to speak, doomed by his name. In Gogol-the-fatalist, the name already encourages and determines the fate of a character.

RETURN TO THE PLOT 3: KHALIAVA

It will be recalled that earlier I promised that the name Khaliava, the last of the three seminarists who started out from Kiev together one fine day to begin their summer vacation, would provide the final clue to the story's meaning. To recall, "Viy" does not end with Thomas's death. Although in the rough drafts the story ends with Thomas's death in the church, Gogol later added a new finale: Tiberius and Khaliava meet to grieve over Thomas's death. At the end of this meeting, the very drunk Khaliava, and this is the last sentence in the story, "cautiously got up from the table, and, lurching right and left, went to hide in a remote spot in the rough grass; from force of habit, however, he did not forget to carry off the sole of an old boot that was lying on the bench." This sole episode is of course hilarious. Still, was there only a comic purpose in adding a new finale to "Viy"? As almost always in Gogol, the comic is not only comic. In Russian, *khaliava* is a word for the top section of a high boot *minus* the sole. Thus, in picking up a sole, Khaliava-the-personage, so to speak, makes himself complete and draws the last circle of the story. Although this is deeply encoded, Gogol nevertheless allows it to be understood. From this final hint we can reconstruct the personal code of the story: that, at every level, "Viy" is about bringing together what has been kept apart—son from mother, Ukraine from Rome, and various androgynous pairs.

As for the names in Gogol, they are like shadows in Plato's famous cave: if we are able to see through them we will discover a parallel world.

Conclusion: Musings on Modifications of Exorcism

I HAVE USED examples drawn from the work of Pushkin, Lermontov, and Gogol to illustrate that what I call a psychological dominant of an author of this type—a prose writer with a transcendent poetic mentality—can be traced by using two things simultaneously: the author's texts and the author's life. In other words, it can be found at the crossroads of intertextuality and biographism. As this is not a book of literary theory but rather a collection of speculative essays, I have thus far avoided speaking about the theoretical possibilities inherent in my approach. Nevertheless, if only because I teach in a literature department and my colleagues would find it strange were I to avoid the topic entirely, I would like to take a little bit of space to muse on these implications. Because the tasks of the biographical and intertextual schools differ significantly from mine, let us turn to their essence as I understand it. In so doing, we will try to see at which point(s) our three roads meet and at which they go in other directions.

The difference between biographism and intertextuality was cogently described by Joseph Brodsky in his speech about Thomas Hardy, "Wooing the Inanimate." Brodsky says:

> True, the literature on Thomas Hardy the poet is fairly negligible. There are two or three full-length studies; they are essentially doctoral-dissertations-turned-books. There are also two or three biographies of the man, including one he penned himself, though it bears his wife's name on the cover. They are worth reading, especially the last *if you believe—as I expect you do—that the artist's life holds the key for the understanding of his work. If you believe the opposite, you won't lose much by giving them a miss, since we are here to address his work* [emphasis added].[1]

Indeed, biographism insists that the artist's life "holds the key" to his work, that the events of the author's life are reflected in his or her production. To my mind, one of the best examples of precisely this approach was given by George Orwell in his essay "Charles Dickens." Orwell writes:

Conclusion

> The one detailed account of child labour that he [Dickens] gives is the description in *David Copperfield* of little David washing bottles in Murdstone and Grinby's warehouse. This, of course, is autobiography. Dickens himself, at the age of ten, had worked in Warren's blacking factory in the Strand, very much as he describes it here. It was a terribly bitter memory to him, partly because he felt the whole incident to be discreditable to his parents, and he even concealed it from his wife till long after they were married. Looking back on this period, he says in *David Copperfield:*
>
> > "It is a matter of some surprise to me, even now, that I can have been so easily thrown away at such an age. A child of excellent abilities and with strong powers of observation, quick, eager, delicate, and soon hurt bodily or mentally, it seems wonderful to me that nobody should have made any sign in my behalf. But none was made; and I became, at ten years old, a little labouring hind in the service of Murdstone and Grinby."
>
> ... Obviously it is not David Copperfield who is speaking, it is Dickens himself.[2]

It is difficult to argue with Orwell: *David Copperfield* is indeed a cry of anguish. Dickens, who survived exactly the same life troubles as his hero, cries out with two voices here. It is also true that the novel grows out of the facts of Dickens's life. Orwell's interpretation of *David Copperfield* is that it *is* such a *result,* and biographism is concerned with literary works as the results of an author's life. Again, there is no need to dispute whether this is true: everything that an artist creates has of course a direct connection with either how he or she lives or at least how he or she feels (or has been feeling) at a given moment. The task of biographism is to find those connections, to provide us with them.

However, in interpreting a text in this way biographism changes neither the *meaning* of a literary work nor its *value*. *David Copperfield* is a great novel even without our knowledge of the facts of Dickens's life. It is already an *overt* cry of Dickens's soul, though it would probably be less powerful a cry had its author suffered less. By *overt* I mean that the author is open about his or her pain (or joy) before the audience; the author does not try to conceal this pain but rather readily demonstrates how he or she feels. Although *David Copperfield* is very personal, and although the novel is a struggle, it is still not a coded struggle on the part of Dickens. It is not Dickens's exorcism simply because he shares the suffering with his audience. Dickens probably tried, while writing, to overcome his pain, and the pain is obvious to us.

Hence, the shared and the different emerge between finding a personal code and the biographical approach. *Shared*: like the latter, the former does not search for the meaning of the literary work. The biographist believes (as I do) that elements of an author's biography, or the facts of his or her life, might allow us to recognize a point—a psychological dominant of the author—out of which a textual result can come. Thus, the facts of Dickens's life can lead us to begin speculating as to whether in his case a psychological dominant would be, let us say, his childhood trauma. *Different:* when biographical facts are directly and overtly paralleled in the literary work they still do not speak about his or her secret personal code, that is, the concealed personal struggle with an author's fears or for his or her secret wishes. In order to discover this code we need more evidence, that is, other texts.

Other texts—this is the point in which intertextuality overlaps with my concern. *Common:* in order to find out we need not just a single text but other text(s) of the author. As Harold Bloom pointed out:

> All criticisms that call themselves primary vacillate between tautology—in which the poem is and means itself—and reduction—in which the poem means something that is not itself a poem. Antithetical criticism must begin by denying both tautology and reduction, a denial best delivered by the assertion that the *meaning* of a poem can only be a poem, but *another poem—a poem not itself* [first emphasis added].[3]

Omry Ronen, another authority on intertextuality, writes in reference to Mandelstam:

> A decoding of the *meaning* [smysla] of many "key" lexico-semantic units in the compound parts of one structure is impossible without analyses of their *full context*, that is, sum total of the cases of this or that use of words . . . [first emphasis added].[4]

Different: although various trends in intertextuality approach the text/texts relationship differently, all of them share the point that text itself is sufficient as the agent of the meaning. My point is that some elements of text cannot be discovered solely by textual analysis. I look for the nexus of life + text.

However, Igor Smirnov goes a bit further than other scholars:

> . . . intertextuality is a component of a broad generic concept, so to speak, inter . . . ality, which indicates that the *meaning* [smysl] of a literary work—entirely or partially—is formed through the instrumentality of references to another text that can be found either *among the works of the same author, or in the adjacent art, or in the adjacent discourse, or in the previous literature* [emphasis added].[5]

Conclusion

Different: what is to be found out? As we have seen from the preceding quotations, intertextuality is concerned with discovering the meaning of a text via its combinations with other texts. When this meaning is found it automatically raises the value of a literary work. My interest—a personal code of the author—does not pretend to change the meaning of a given text/texts. It is, so to speak, a text "extra." When this "extra" is found, it does not add to the value or change the meaning of the text as a literary work.

Common: this "extra" can be called, in Smirnov's terms, an "inter . . . ality," because it exists as some *inner reality* in the text. It must be found, if we use Smirnov's term, by employing "an adjacent discourse." In our case, however, it would mean only the author's life as a text.

Different: while employing various texts of the author as well as his or her life as a text, I am searching for an author's personal code, that is, that which is meaningful only for the author and not for the text.

Let me sum up then. In order to find a psychological dominant of the author we use the facts of his or her life (overlap with biographism). The facts of his or her life are just another text (outside the purview of biographism; overlap with intertextuality). In combination with more written texts of the same author or those of another author (overlap with intertextuality) we find his or her personal code, or exorcism of his or her psychological dominant (outside the purview of both biographism and intertextuality).

The personal code is neither a text's meaning nor its value (thus different from intertextuality), nor a key to the author's work in general (thus different from biographism). It is concealed and not overt, although that which is overt (overlap with biographism) can but does not necessarily lead us to an author's psychological dominant, that is, the first track to his or her personal code.

MODIFICATIONS OF EXORCISM

We are almost at the end of this book. Many types and cases of authorial exorcism have by necessity been excluded. Exorcism, as understood here, is not a literary device but a dimension of the creative process and one of its results. At the same time, I by no means insist that it is a Klondike for the scholar, although it does not do any harm to stake a claim to it. Exorcism is that psychological territory which is private, and any trespass does not automatically signify that you have found gold. However, some cases of exorcism are more apparent than those I have attempted to solve in this book, and thus more inviting. Let us look at just one.

In 1989, Joseph Brodsky (1940–96) wrote the poem "Fin-de-siècle," which starts:

Writing as Exorcism

> Век скоро кончится, но раньше кончусь я.
> Это, боюсь, не вопрос чутья.
> Скорее - влияние небытия
> на бытие; охотника, так сказать, на дичь,—
> будь то сердечная мышца или кирпич. . . .[6]

> The century will be soon over, but I'll be over even sooner.
> This, I am afraid, is not a question of intuition.
> Rather—it is the influence of non-existence
> on existence; of a hunter on his prey, so to speak,—
> whether it be the heart-muscle or a brick.

The first line sounds like some kind of self-prophecy: the poet—sadly—predicts that he will not reach the end of the century. Moreover, it is clear that he believes in at least something (nonexistence) that decides the limits of our lifetime (existence). He also believes that his knowledge of the fact that he will die before the century is over is not a matter of intuition but—in his case—the inevitability of the laws imposed on the existence by nonexistence. Thus, he believes in destiny, and that is why it makes no difference what the cause of his death might be: his bad heart or even a brick that might fall down from somewhere (the Russian idiom *kirpich upal s kryshi*—"a brick fell from the roof"—is usually connected to a sudden death).

If, as Brodsky himself claims, the poet's intuition about imminent death is not the cause of such a statement, then what is? A coquetry with fate? A prophetic insight? The melancholy assertion of a visionary? But why write about it? Even a stoic or just a philosophically minded person, though he or she is somehow tranquil that death will come, would not, so to speak, bring it upon himself or herself as Brodsky does by saying that it will happen before the century is over. And he unquestionably feared death: one of Brodsky's famous verses—"смерть—это то, что происходит с другими" (death is something that happens to others)—is sufficient evidence of this.

Thus, that which looks like a self-prophecy—something that nobody, including the poet, wants to come true—is a pure exorcism. He performs it in order to get rid of his fear, or, using a high-flown style, to persuade nonexistence to spare him—at least till the end of the century, even despite his weak heart. The fact that the exorcism failed—Brodsky died in 1996 and it is not my task here to discuss "other factors," that is, metaphysical ones as well as intuition which Brodsky here denies—does not mean that his goal was not to avoid such a failure.

When I said that the preceding example is a more apparent case of exorcism, I wanted to emphasize that in poetry exorcism often takes the shape of a prayer, which does not fully conceal but rather reveals the wishes of the individual who prays. Thus, Pushkin's "Please, God, do not let me go insane . . ." is a model prayer and a kind of exorcism, too, though an overt one. In Brodsky's poem, which is not quite as openly revealing as Pushkin's, it is hoped that the concept of nonexistence will pay heed. A concealed prayer—specifically in poetry—is a modification of exorcism. Not for nothing is the Devil cast out by prayer in classic exorcism.

Another possible modification of exorcism is its semiconscious origin. And the example I want to give is also from Pushkin.

In 1831, one of Pushkin's least productive years (only six poems), he composed the notorious "To the Slanderers of Russia," a fierce odic comment on the Polish uprising of 1830 to 1831—Poland was then a part of the Russian Empire. The poem starts:

> О чем шумите вы, народные витии?
> Зачем анафемой грозите вы России?
> Что возмутило вас? волнения Литвы?
> Оставьте: это спор славян между собою,
> Домашний, старый спор, уж взвешенный судьбою,
> Вопрос, которого не разрешите вы.[7]

> Why are you so noisy, oh people's orators?
> Why are you threatening Russia with anathema?
> What stirred you up? the agitation in Lithuania [Poland]?
> Drop it!—this an argument of the Slavs between themselves,
> A domestic, old argument, that has already been weighed by fate,
> A problem which you cannot solve.

"You" here are those French deputies and journalists who sympathized with the uprising and were demanding that their government begin an armed intervention in the conflict. In addition to the poem, Pushkin even wrote a letter to Benkendorf, the chief of the Russian secret police and his flagrant ill-wisher, in order, most probably, to reach the tsar's attention directly. "Embittered Europe attacks Russia not with arms," wrote Pushkin, "but with rabid everyday slander.—Constitutional governments want peace, while young generations, troubled by the press, demand war."[8]

Straight away, Pushkin wrote two more poems dedicated to the same uprising. One, "The Anniversary of Borodino," is not so much about the celebrated battle with Napoleon near Moscow as about the Russian suppression of the Polish uprising:

> Сбылось—и в день Бородина
> Вновь наши вторглись знамена
> В проломы падшей вновь Варшавы;

> И Польша, как бегущий полк,
> Во прах бросает стяг кровавый—
> И бунт раздавленный умолк.⁹

> It happened—on the day of Borodino
> our standards again broke through
> the breaches of Warsaw fallen again;
> and Poland, like a fleeing regiment,
> drops its blood-stained banner into the dust—
> and the crushed mutiny lapses into silence.

It seems that Pushkin is personally injured by the rebellion, for he just cannot stop writing on it. In another poem, on the anniversary of the graduation from his beloved Lycée—a sacred topic for Pushkin—he uses the same iambic tetrameter as in the Borodino poem (metric monotony is generally a sign of a certain psychological inertia) and again touches on the uprising:

> Давно ль, друзья? Но двадцать лет
> Тому прошло; и что же вижу?
> Того царя в живых уж нет;
> Мы жгли Москву; был плен Парижу;
> Угас в тюрьме Наполеон;
> Воскресла греков древних слава;
> С престола пал другой Бурбон;
> Отбунтовала вновь Варшава.¹⁰

> Was it long ago, my friends? Already twenty years
> have passed since; and what do I see?
> That tsar is gone;
> we burned Moscow; Paris was captured;
> Napoleon's light went out in prison;
> the ancient glory of the Greeks was revived;
> another Bourbon fell from his throne;
> Warsaw mutinied again.

As it happens, Pushkin excluded this stanza—initially the second—from the poem's final version. Still, the obsession with the Polish topic is present: three of six poems written in 1831 touch on it. Why? I am not going to discuss either Pushkin's political or other social reasons for writing them. There are plenty of these. What is evident, though, is the fact that Pushkin was touched *personally* and definitely confused.

The year 1832 was not very productive either: all together eight poems.

Pushkin begins it with a strange poem, "And we went further—and fear embraced me . . ." ("I dale my poshli—I strakh obnial menia . . ."). This poem is a variation on Dante, in terza rima, about Pushkin's descent to Hell, and, of course, about the sinners' sufferings there. What is important is that *fear* is the feeling that Pushkin pointed out in the very beginning. In other words, the poem is written out of fear. Of what? For the moment, I will skip the answer.

In 1833, Pushkin wrote *The Bronze Horseman*. In this *poema*—among other things—he describes the Petersburg flood of 1824 and discourses upon the ambiguous role of Peter the Great in Russian history. In both cases, after his description of the flood and that of Etienne Maurice Falconet's famous monument to Peter, Pushkin uses footnotes referring to Adam Mickiewicz (1798–1855). About the flood he notes: "Mickiewicz described the day before the flood in the beautiful verses in one of his best poems—Oleszkiewicz. It is a pity, though, that his description is not correct. There was no snow that day—the Neva was not covered with ice. Our description is more accurate, although it lacks the bright colors of the Polish poet." About the monument he writes: "For more, see the description of the monument in Mickiewicz."[11] The name of the great Polish poet thus comes up twice in the footnotes, and there are only five of them in the entire *poema*. Pushkin's intonation in relation to him is both respectful and defensive, if not obsequious. Why?

It is well known that Pushkin, in his footnotes, aimed at the series of anti-Russian poems on Petersburg by Mickiewicz as well as his *poema Dziady (Forefathers)*.[12] In the *Fragment*, an addition to its third part (both were published the year before, in 1832), Mickiewicz indeed slings mud at Peter the Great and at Russians in general (lines 203–14):

>
> Piotr zaprowadził bębny i bagnety,
> Postawił turmy, urządził kadety,
> Kazał na dworze tańczyć menuety
> I do towarzystw gwałtem wwiodł kobiety;
> I na granicach poosadzał straże,
> I łańcuchami pozamykał porty,
> Utworzył senat, szpiegi, dygnitarze,
> Odkupy wódek, czyny i paszporty;—
> Ogolił, umył i ustroił chłopa,
> Dał mu broń w ręce, kieszeń narublował,
> I zadziwiona krzyknęła Europa:
> "Car Piotr Rosyją ucywilizował."
>
> Peter introduced drums and bayonets,
> built prisons, established cadets,

Writing as Exorcism

> gave the order to dance minuets at court
> and quickly brought women into society;
> and put frontier guards on the borders,
> and closed his ports with chains,
> established the senate, spies, grandees,
> opened vodka distilleries, ranks, and passports;
> shaved, washed, and dressed the peasant,
> put arms in his hands, roubles in his pocket,
> and Europe exclaimed in amazement:
> "Tsar Peter has civilized Russia."

On Falconet's monument of Peter, Mickiewicz sarcastically comments (lines 57–63):

> Car Piotr wypuścił rumakowi wodze,
> Widać, że leciał tratując po drodze,
> Od razu wskoczył aż na sam brzeg skały.
> Już koń szalony wzniósł w górę kopyta,
> Car go nie trzyma, koń wędzidłem zgrzyta,
> Zgadniesz, że spadnie i pryśnie w kawały.
>
> Od wieku stoi, skacze, lecz nie spada,

> Tsar Peter gave the argamak the reins,
> it seems that it flew, trampling, over the road,
> and jumped at once to the very edge of the rock.
> The violent horse has already lifted up its hooves,
> the tsar does not hold it back, the horse bites the bridle,
> you think that it will fall down and break into pieces.
>
> Always remain, galloping, just don't fall down,

I have quoted both pieces from *Dziady* in order to emphasize two equally significant points. First, Mickiewicz is definitely biased when demonstrating his hatred. He has, however, all the right in the world to show his partiality: he is a Polish patriot, as much as Pushkin—with certain reservations—is a Russian one. The second point to be emphasized is that Pushkin is obviously irritated by Mickiewicz's comments. But, and this is very unusual for him, Pushkin nevertheless holds himself back and does not, in his turn, come down upon the caustic Pole, at least not openly.

Moreover, in the same year as *The Bronze Horseman* Pushkin translates two poems by Mickiewicz of 1827 and 1828: "Trzech Budrysów (ballada litewska)"—"Stary Budrys trzech synów, tęgich jak sam Litwinów . . ."—and

Conclusion

"Czaty (ballada ukrainska)"—"Z ogrodowej altany wojewoda zdyszany..." Pushkin gives them his own titles: "Budrys and his Sons" ("Budrys i ego synov'ia") and "The Voivoda" ("Voevoda").

In 1834, Pushkin—one after another—writes a poem that this time is directly anti-Mickiewiczian and translates from French *The Songs of the Western Slavs,* a famous hoax of Mérimée. In the introduction to the latter he seems to have immediately retreated from the previous poem, characterizing Mickiewicz as "a perspicacious and shrewd critic of Slavic poetry." The poem, though, is important to us here because it is Pushkin's response to Mickiewicz's poetic epistle of 1832 "To My Russian Friends," which—in its turn—was the Polish poet's angry reaction to Pushkin's anti-Polish poetic attacks. Pushkin's poem goes:

> Он между нами жил
> Средь племени ему чужого; злобы
> В душе своей к нам не питал, и мы
> Его любили. Мирный, благосклонный,
> Он посещал беседы наши. С ним
> Делились мы и чистыми мечтами
> И песнями (он вдохновен был свыше
> И свысока взирал на жизнь). Нередко
> Он говорил о временах грядущих,
> Когда народы, распри позабыв,
> В великую семью соединятся.
> Мы жадно слушали поэта. Он
> Ушел на запад—и благословеньем
> Его мы проводили. Но теперь
> Наш мирный гость нам стал врагом—и ядом
> Стихи свои, в угоду черни буйной,
> Он напояет. Издали до нас
> Доходит голос злобного поэта,
> Знакомый голос!... боже! освяти
> В нем сердце правдою твоей и миром,
> И возврати ему...[13]

> He lived among us,
> a tribe alien to him; in his soul
> he did not nourish any anger against us, and we
> loved him. Peaceful, gracious,
> he visited our discussions. With him
> we shared our pure dreams
> and songs (he was inspired from above
> and observed life loftily). Quite often

he spoke about those future times
when peoples, having forgotten their feuds,
will unite in a large family.
We listened to the poet greedily. He
left for the West—and we saw him off
with our blessing. But now
our peaceful guest has become our enemy—and to please the wild mob
he fills his poems with poison.
The voice of the vindictive poet
comes to us from afar,
a familiar voice! . . . Lord! sanctify
his heart with your veracity and harmony,
and give him back . . .

Indeed, after he had been expelled for political reasons from Vilno, Lithuania, to Russia, Mickiewicz had been a relatively close friend of Pushkin's for five years, from 1824 to 1829. In 1829, Mickiewicz left Petersburg for Paris, where he spent most of the rest of his life writing and teaching survey courses on Slavic literatures. In "To My Russian Friends," Mickiewicz's response to the suppression of the Polish uprising as well as to Pushkin's anti-uprising poems, he had written: "Now I empty out to the world a goblet with poison. Caustic and burning hot is the brininess of my utterance."

Although Pushkin mentions the "poisoned poems" of the Polish bard, his otherwise utterly sad poem on Mickiewicz is more a gentle prayer for his "soul" than a verbal vendetta—a genre in which Pushkin was a real virtuoso when he wanted to use it.

Why did he spare his assailant?

First of all, for all his attacks Mickiewicz was still a friend, and Pushkin was extremely tender toward his friends. Indeed, he probably valued the institution of friendship more than anything else. When a friendship seemingly fell apart—as was the case with Mickiewicz—Pushkin's reaction was extreme bitterness. In verses not included in the final version of the poem, Pushkin directly calls Mickiewicz his friend:

Мы встретились, и были мы друзья,
Хоть наши племена и враждовали.[14]

We met, and became friends,
Although our tribes were enemies.

It is noteworthy that after Pushkin was killed Mickiewicz wrote a deeply sympathetic obituary and signed it "one of Pushkin's friends."

Conclusion

Second, Pushkin—deep inside—most likely knew that Mickiewicz was right to react to his anti-Polish poems the way he did. Even for Pushkin, Mickiewicz's rage was, so to speak, fair. Although "To the Slanderers of Russia" and the two other anti-Polish poems of 1831 were probably sincere, Pushkin without a doubt could have predicted that they would infuriate his Polish friend, who was already in emigration. Pushkin definitely tries to mend the matter already in 1832: he translates Mickiewicz's poems. Interestingly enough, these poems had been written in 1827 and 1828, that is, at the height of Mickiewicz's friendship with Pushkin. It seems that Pushkin—by the very fact of his translations—wants Mickiewicz to recall those happy and "peaceful" years. Nevertheless, Mickiewicz does not keep silent in the face of Pushkin's anti-Polish philippics and in the same year, 1832, writes the malicious "To My Russian Friends" and the relevant sections of his *Dziady*. With a sense of sad inevitability, Pushkin answers both with the footnotes to his *poema* (nevertheless an indication that he was thinking frequently about Mickiewicz and, probably, about his personal guilt before the Polish poet) and, again sorrowfully, with the verses about "the vindictive poet."

If we attempt to qualify all of Pushkin's moves toward/against Mickiewicz, we will probably conclude that they form another psychological dominant of the Russian poet—his guilty "Polish" conscience—with which he *overtly*, that is, quite *consciously*, struggles. Where is the exorcism then?

When I promised an example of *semiconscious* exorcism, that is, another modification of the *conscious* ones described in this book, I had in mind the mysterious variation on Dante with which Pushkin started 1832. To recall, it begins with fear, which "embraces" the author who descends to Hell. In Russian, "Hell" is *Ad,* and this word appears twice in the poem's two short parts. The poem *is* written out of fear—not out of fear of some fictitious future Inferno, but of present punishment in *Ad.* If we guess that Pushkin was deeply troubled that his anti-Polish poems would cost him his friendship with Mickiewicz, it does not seem impossible that by *Ad* Pushkin meant "Adam," the first name of Mickiewicz. Pushkin, it seems, feels pangs of conscience. He realizes that he—on a personal level—has betrayed his Polish friend, and he exorcises his guilty conscience by sending himself to *Ad,* punishing himself by observing there the suffering of other sinners. *Ad* = Adam is Pushkin's personal code in the poem, and the poem is the exorcism he performs in order to redeem his guilt. Why do I call this exorcism semiconscious?

Pushkin left no evidence, either in his poems or in his letters, of repentance for his anti-Polish poems. Thus, the fact that Pushkin realized his guilt before Mickiewicz cannot be proved by anything but the *"ad"*-anagram of the latter's name in the poem as well as the puzzling appearance of the poem itself in a group of works following the anti-Polish poems and those writings that were directly connected with Mickiewicz. Because those works, as well as the very fact of their appearance, are overtly ambiguous, that is, partially apologetic and partially hostile, we can conclude that Pushkin *was* confused. All this suggests that the anagram is indeed possible, although it cannot be said for sure that Pushkin intentionally used it.

Mickiewicz read Pushkin's poem about him—"the vindictive poet"—only after the latter's death. Pushkin's friend A. Turgenev, who gave the poem his own title, "A Voice from the Other World," put it on Mickiewicz's pulpit at the university in Paris.[15] Ironically to some extent, Pushkin—precisely in relation to Mickiewicz—had already experienced this "other world" during his lifetime.

The two examples given here in conclusion are modifications of literary exorcism: a concealed prayer and a semiconscious one. They do not, of course, exhaust the implications of exorcism for biographical, intertextual, or aesthetic appreciation. Even if authors do not want us to reveal their personal codes or simply do not care whether we make our attempts to crack them, we, while reading their works, are usually puzzled with so many questions that sometimes exorcism's "pick"—a tool for a forcible entry—is just what we need, another professional tool of setting the door ajar. For the doors of authors' personal secrets do not open by themselves; that happens only in Hollywood when a defeated devil leaves the place.

Notes

INTRODUCTION
1. For Boggs, the entire exchange was the work of art; thus he insisted on getting change for his drawings of currency. See Lawrence Weschler, *Boggs: A Comedy of Values*, Chicago, 1999.
2. Tolstoy, p. 528.

CHAPTER ONE
1. Sosnora, p. 31.
2. Kulish, p. 43.
3. Quoted in Gogol, *Sobranie sochinenii v deviati tomakh*, vol. 7, p. 525.
4. About this, see ibid., pp. 521, 525.
5. Ibid., p. 66.
6. Gogol, *Dead Souls*, p. 1.
7. Tarkovsky, p. 202.
8. Ibid., p. 206.
9. Ibid., p. 203.
10. Ibid., p. 203.
11. Ibid., p. 216.
12. Ibid., p. 213.
13. Bloom, pp. 10–11.

CHAPTER TWO
Epigraph: Baratynsky, p. 175.
1. Zhukovsky, pp. 154–155.
2. Pushkin, *Eugene Onegin*, trans. Charles Johnston, Harmondsworth, N.Y., 1979. All further references to *Eugene Onegin* will be to this edition.
3. Baratynsky, pp. 176–77.
4. Veresaev, *Pushkin v zhizni*, vol. 1, p. 294.
5. Ibid., p. 295.
6. *Entsiklopediia sueverii*, pp. 123, 410.

7. Ibid., pp. 142–43.
8. Ibid., p. 75.
9. Ibid., p. 181.
10. Ibid., p. 170.
11. Veresaev, *Pushkin v zhizni*, vol. 2, p. 89.
12. Ibid., p. 95.
13. *Entsiklopediia sueverii*, p. 402.
14. Veresaev, *Pushkin v zhizni*, vol. 2, p. 128.
15. Derzhavin, pp. 52–54.
16. Gorlin, p. 336.
17. Lotman, *Izbrannye stat'i*, p. 400.
18. Veresaev, *Pushkin v zhizni*, vol. 1, p. 347.
19. Ibid., p. 218.
20. Ibid., p. 187.
21. Ibid., p. 384.
22. Ibid., p. 404.
23. Lotman, *Besedy o russkoi kul'ture*, p. 137.
24. Karatygin, pp. 21–22.
25. *Legendy i mify o Pushkine*, p. 250.
26. Tsiavlovsky, p. 190.
27. *Pushkin v vospominaniiakh sovremennikov*, pp. 5–6.
28. *Legendy i mify o Pushkine*, p. 252.
29. Veresaev, *Pushkin v zhizni*, vol. 2, p. 167.
30. Veresaev, *Pushkin v zhizni*, vol. 1, p. 355.
31. Ibid., p. 342.
32. Ibid., p. 350.
33. Ibid., p. 365.
34. Veresaev, *Pushkin v zhizni*, vol. 2, pp. 291–92.
35. Ibid., p. 198.
36. Pushkin, *Complete Prose Fiction*, p. 230.
37. Among the most recent articles on the numerology in *The Queen of Spades*, see Rosen, Leighton.
38. Lotman, *Izbrannye stat'i*, vol. 2, p. 389.
39. Emerson.
40. Eichenbaum, *Stat'i o Lermontove*, p. 253.
41. For a further discussion of this tendency in Pushkin, see Gasparov, pp. 249–51.
42. Pushkin, *Complete Prose Fiction*, p. 233.
43. Veresaev, *Pushkin v zhizni*, vol. 2, p. 192.
44. Ibid.
45. Ibid., p. 194.
46. The connection to Bunyan is discussed in the notes to Pushkin, *Sobranie sochinenii v desiati tomakh*, vol. 2, p. 608.

47. Ibid., p. 239.
48. Ibid.
49. *Entsiklopediia sueverii*, p. 245.
50. Veresaev, *Pushkin v zhizni*, vol. 2, p. 241.
51. Ibid.
52. Ibid., p. 243.
53. Ibid., p. 248.
54. Ibid., p. 252.
55. Pushkin, *Complete Prose Fiction*, pp. 232–33.
56. Veresaev, *Pushkin v zhizni*, vol. 1, p. 330.
57. Veresaev, *Pushkin v zhizni*, vol. 2, p. 196.
58. Pushkin, *Complete Prose Fiction*, p. 232.
59. Dahl, p. 110.
60. Plutarch, p. 575.
61. Veresaev, *Pushkin v zhizni*, vol. 2, pp. 360–61.
62. Ibid., p. 462.
63. Ibid., p. 463.
64. Pasternak's letter to Eugene M. Kaiden, August 22, 1958. Quoted in Pasternak.
65. Lermontov, *A Hero of Our Time*, p. 182.
66. Pushkin, *Complete Prose Fiction*, p. 211.
67. Lermontov, *A Hero of Our Time*, p. 183.
68. Belinsky, p. 261.
69. Pushkin, *Complete Prose Fiction*, pp. 218–19.
70. As one of the first Lermontov scholars, P. Viskovaty claimed that "The Fatalist" was "copied from an incident that happened at the Cossack settlement of Chervlennaia with Khastatov [Lermontov's uncle]. At least, the episode in which Pechorin rushes into the hut of a drunk and enraged Cossack happened to Khastatov; all this I heard from A. P. Shan-Girei. Khokhriakov says that he was told by S. A. Raevsky that 'The Fatalist' is an actual incident in which Lermontov himself took part together with Mongo Stolypin." (Viskovaty, p. 263)
71. Lermontov, *A Hero of Our Time*, pp. 183–84.
72. Ibid., p. 186.
73. Quoted in Manuilov, p. 255.
74. Ibid., p. 254.
75. Lermontov, *A Hero of Our Time*, p. 165.
76. Ibid., p. 167.
77. Ibid., p. 163.
78. Ibid., p. 163.
79. Ibid., p. 185.
80. Ibid., p. 164.
81. Ibid., p. 166.

82. Ibid., pp. 209–10.
83. *Entsiklopediia sueverii*, p. 432.
84. Ibid., p. 433.
85. Lermontov, *Sochineniia v 6 tomakh*, vol. 6, p. 456.
86. Manuilov, p. 255.
87. Lermontov, *Sochineniia v 6 tomakh*, vol. 2, p. 167.
88. Lermontov, *A Hero of Our Time*, p. 182.
89. Viskovaty, p. 346.
90. Sosnora, pp. 31, 32, 34.

CHAPTER THREE

Epigraph: Back panel of the box for a toy, Wind-Up Running Nose, Item #10071. © 1995 Accoutrements.

1. Rostand, pp. 39–41.
2. Veresaev, *Gogol v zhizni*, p. 185.
3. Though bound to Gogol for a long time, stories about noses lost and regained were quite popular in the literature of 1820 to 1830. For more, see Vinogradov.
4. Morson, pp. 200–39; Karlinsky, p. 129.
5. Gogol, *The Complete Tales*, p. 228.
6. Annensky, pp. 7, 8.
7. Yermakov, pp. 155–98. About this analysis Simon Karlinsky writes sarcastically: "As could have been expected, Dr. Yermakov had a field day with this story, seeing phallic symbolism not only in the major's missing nose and the barber's loaf of bread, but also in the nose's entry into the cathedral, which takes place on March 25, the Feast of the Annunciation." (Karlinsky, p. 130)
8. *Razviazka* in Russian suggests two ways of its understanding: as actual "final" and, as it might have been translated also, as "The Final Inspector General."
9. Gogol, *Sobranie sochinenii v deviati tomakh*, vol. 4, pp. 462–63.
10. Vinitsky, p. 200.
11. Though a great admirer of Karlinsky's work on Gogol, I disagree with his statement that "like all works of authentically surrealistic art, 'The Nose' stubbornly resists paraphrase or conversion into an allegory" (Karlinsky, p. 130).
12. Gogol, *Sobranie sochinenii v deviati tomakh*, vol. 3, p. 30.
13. *Russkaia elegiia XVIII-nachala XX veka*, p. 341.
14. All quotations from *Dead Souls* are marked by chapter and page number from Nikolai Gogol, *Dead Souls: The Reavey Translation*, ed. George Gibian, New York, 1985.
15. Pushkin, *Eugene Onegin*, p. 80.

16. Lotman, *Roman A. S. Pushkina "Evgenii Onegin": Kommentarii,* p. 228.

17. Pushkin, *Eugene Onegin,* p. 150.

18. For more meaning, see Dahl, vol. 4, p. 604.

19. Gogol, *The Complete Tales,* pp. 219–20.

20. Ibid., p. 237.

21. I quote Nabokov's translation in Nabokov, *Lectures on Literature,* pp. 257–58.

22. Veresaev, *Pushkin v zhizni,* vol. 2, p. 259.

23. Gogol, *Arabesques,* pp. 257–58.

24. In pre-Muslim Arabia, the cult of the moon was paramount, and later Muhammad prohibited the use of any metal but silver in amulets. See the article titled "Moon" in Juan Eduardo Cirlot, *A Dictionary of Symbols,* trans. Jack Sage, New York, 1962.

25. For more, see V. Sokolova, *Vesenne-letnie kalendarnye obriady russkikh, ukraitsev I belorusov. XIX-nachalo XX veka,* Moscow, 1979.

26. Plato, p. 545.

27. Gogol, *Sobranie sochinenii v deviati tomakh,* vol. 6, p. 312.

28. For more, see Efim Etkind, *Russkie poety-perevodchiki ot Trediakovskogo do Pushkina,* Leningrad, 1973; Iurii Levin, *Russkie perevodchiki XIX veka i razvitie khudozhestvennogo perevoda,* Leningrad, 1985.

29. Ariosto, *The Orlando Furioso,* trans. William Stewart Rose, London, 1828. All further citations from Ariosto are from this edition, and marked by volume and canto numbers in the main text.

30. Gogol, *Arabesques,* p. 136.

31. Gogol, *Sobranie sochinenii v deviati tomakh,* vol. 4, p. 486.

32. Annenkov, *Materialy dlia biografii Pushkina,* p. 360.

33. Gogol, *Sobranie sochinenii v deviati tomakh,* vol. 6, pp. 194–95.

34. Ibid., pp. 210–11.

35. Tarasenkov, p. 11.

36. *Gimnaziia vysshykh nauk i litsei kn. Bezborodko,* Petersburg, 1881, p. 198.

37. Gogol, *Sobranie sochinenii v deviati tomakh,* vol. 6, p. 291.

38. Veresaev, *Pushkin v zhizni,* vol. 2, p. 120.

39. Ibid., p. 181.

40. *Pushkin Threefold,* pp. 140–41.

CHAPTER FOUR

Epigraphs: Babkin and Shendetsov, p. 154; Annenkov, *Literaturnye vospominaniia,* p. 67.

1. For more on *Syn Otechestva,* see Kuleshov, pp. 193–94.

2. Gogol, *Sobranie sochinenii v deviati tomakh,* vol. 7, pp. 9–10.

3. Venevitinov, p. 64.
4. Baratynsky, p. 76.
5. Ibid., p. 217.
6. Veresaev, *Gogol v zhizni*, p. 214.
7. Kotliarevsky, p. 23.
8. Veresaev, *Gogol v zhizni*, p. 214.
9. Quoted in Venevitinov, p. 7.
10. Weiskopf, pp. 126–42.
11. Gogol, *Sobranie sochinenii v deviati tomakh*, vol. 8, pp. 71–72.

12. In Symposium, Plato writes about "hermaphrodite": "The three sexes, I may say, arose as follows. The males were descended from the Sun, the females from the Earth, and the hermaphrodites from the Moon, which partakes of either sex . . ." (Plato, p. 543). Thus, the *nus-nos* of Gogol and the androgynous being both belong to the moon.

13. We find an echo of Plato's legend in Ovid's *Metamorphoses* (IV, 271–388), in the story of Hermaphroditus, the beautiful son of Hermes and Aphrodite. (In English literature, this tale became famous after the poem *Salmacis and Hermaphroditus* [1602] by Francis Beaumont.) There, the nymph falls in love with Hermaphroditus and asks the gods to allow her to stay with him forever. The gods unify her with Hermaphroditus in a form of a being that is half man, half woman.

14. Robert A. Maguire, who attaches special importance to the Roman topic in Gogol's writings in his book *Exploring Gogol*, does not, however, mention its presence in *Mirgorod*.

15. Gukovsky, p. 70. All translations in this essay, if the name of translator is not mentioned, are mine.

16. Although in Gogol's time *mir* was written differently, as "мир =" (for "peace") and "мiр" (for "world"), it did not make much difference, for both words are homonyms and thus were pronounced alike. Also, as it was shown by the linguist and historian N. Samsonov, the Russian letter "i" often was used for "и," namely in the thirteenth, fifteenth, sixteenth, and late-seventeenth centuries, when "i" was expelled from the written language (Samsonov, p. 67).

17. It seems that for the first time this "double" meaning of the title *Mirgorod* was pointed out by Vladimir Turbin in his book *Pushkin. Gogol. Lermontov: Ob izuchenii literaturnykh zhanrov* (pp. 171–72). Also, it was mentioned by Richard Peace in his book *The Enigma of Gogol: An Examination of the Writings of N. V. Gogol and Their Place in the Russian Literary Tradition* (p. 30) and then repeated by Viktor Guminsky in his article "'Taras Bulba' v *Mirgorode* i *Arabeskakh*" (pp. 245–47). However, none of the scholars does more than flag these meanings.

18. The palindrome as a device was especially widely used in the Baroque, whose origin in Russian literature was Ukraine (see, for example,

the palindromes of Feofan Prokopovich and Ivan Velichkovskii). In his book *Nikolai Gogol and the Baroque Cultural Heritage,* Georgy Shapiro touches upon, among other Baroque features in Gogol, his playing with words (see the chapter titled "Wordplay"), but not palindromes. And, of course, he is right when writing that "Gogol, whose outstanding receptiveness to language was perhaps enhanced by his being bilingual in Ukrainian and Russian, was undoubtedly familiar with wordplay from his childhood" (Shapiro, p. 227).

19. Also, it is significant that the wording *urbi et orbi* is usually translated into Russian as *Rimu i miru,* that is, in a "palind-roman" form. See Babkin and Shendetsov, pp. 526–27.

20. Gogol, *The Complete Tales,* pp. 8–9.

21. Ibid., p. 186.

22. The scholar of *The Iliad* M. Silk uses the term "duel" for the battle scenes in Homer in his book *Homer: The Iliad,* Cambridge, 1987, p. 43.

23. Gogol, *The Complete Tales,* p. 108.

24. Ibid., p. 181.

25. Gogol, *Arabesques,* p. 101.

26. Gogol, *Sobranie sochinenii v deviati tomakh,* vol. 3, p. 189.

27. Ibid., p. 180.

28. Gogol, *The Complete Tales,* pp. 151, 158.

29. *Gogol from the Twentieth Century,* p. 59.

30. Translation by Robert A. Maguire in *Gogol from the Twentieth Century,* p. 58.

31. Nabokov, *Nikolai Gogol,* p. 73.

32. Mann, p. 115.

33. Kireevsky, p. 226.

34. Though *Dead Souls* is indeed a nationalistic novel, as is proved by the portrayal of as a "bird-troika" in the finale, Kopeykin's story might have another purpose: the sole funny feature of "The Story . . ." remains the fact that Captain Kopeykin was missing an arm and a leg. Kopeykin's leg, on the contrary, is not entirely lost in the song: he just stumbled, and to stumble is a bad omen for Russians; that is why Kopeykin calls his dream a bad one.

35. Gogol, *Dead Souls,* pp. 15–16.

36. "Crazy Piety," *The New Yorker,* September 29, 1997, p. 34.

37. Eichenbaum, "How 'The Overcoat' Is Made," p. 275. For a discussion of Gogol's attitude toward personal names, see ibid., pp. 273–74.

38. Plato, pp. 368, 370.

39. Plutarch, p. 804.

40. Suetonius, pp. 43–44.

41. Gogol, *The Complete Tales,* p. 142. Here, I have revised the translation at the beginning of the citation. "He stood up and looked into her face

(there was the glow of sunrise, and the golden domes of the Kiev churches were gleaming in the distance): before him . . ." is how it is in the original translation, although there Thomas looks not into the witch's face, but into her eyes, and then Gogol puts a colon, not round brackets, which hints at what exactly Thomas sees in them.

42. Gogol, *The Complete Tales*, p. 149.
43. Ibid., p. 150.
44. Plato, p. 364.
45. Plutarch, p. 604.
46. Ibid., p. 817.
47. Gogol, *The Complete Tales*, p. 158.
48. Ibid., p. 159.
49. Ibid., p. 161.
50. Stilman, p. 376.
51. Gogol, *The Complete Tales*, pp. 140–41.
52. To recall, Gogol used this same Medusa effect in the "dumb scene" of *The Inspector General*.
53. *Gogol from the Twentieth Century*, p. 377.
54. Karlinsky, p. 101.
55. Veresaev, *Gogol v zhizni*, p. 40. Veresaev has his doubts about Gogol's mother's age when she had him (he speculates she was already eighteen), although officially—that is, as Gogol knew it—she was then around sixteen. She married Gogol's father at age fourteen.
56. Veresaev, *Gogol v zhizni*, p. 36.
57. Ibid., p. 57.
58. Ibid., p. 59.
59. The fact that this situation of devil *versus* devil when they do not recognize each other exists in Gogol as typical can be proven by its numerous repetitions in *Dead Souls*. Thus, to name only one, Chichikov, always a smart buyer, is suddenly cheated and buys a dead female soul, one that is absolutely "useless": in order to sell him one more dead serf, the landowner Sobakevich changed on paper the regular female name Elizaveta Vorobey, Elizabeth the Sparrow, to the nonexistent (but masculine) Elizavet. The explanation of why Chichikov, invincible before, was easily cheated linguistically this time is directly connected with the Gogolian devil-versus-devil topic. And once more, we are able to figure out this topic only if we know what this or that name in Gogol typifies. Here, Chichikov, himself a sparrow, is "defeated" by another sparrow, a name, among others, for the petty devil in Gogol.
60. In his *Dictionary*, Vladimir Dahl says that a sparrow "chikaet" (vol. 4, p. 604).
61. See Gogol, *Sobranie sochinenii v deviati tomakh*, vol. 9, p. 667.
62. Robbins, p. 25.

CONCLUSION
1. Brodsky, *On Grief and Reason*, p. 314.
2. Orwell, p. 61.
3. Bloom, p. 70.
4. Ronen, pp. 370–71.
5. Smirnov, *Porozhdenie interteksta*, p. 11.
6. Brodsky, *Chast' rechi: Izbrannye stikhi 1962–1989*, p. 506.
7. Pushkin, *Sobranie sochinenii v desiati tomakh*, vol. 2, p. 269.
8. Ibid., p. 598.
9. Ibid., pp. 271–72.
10. Ibid., p. 600.
11. Pushkin, *Sobranie sochinenii v desiati tomakh*, vol. 3, p. 268.
12. For more, see Lednicki.
13. Pushkin, *Sobranie sochinenii v desiati tomakh*, vol. 2, p. 316.
14. Ibid., p. 604.
15. Ibid.

Works Cited

Annenkov, Pavel. *Literaturnye vospominaniia*. Moscow, 1989.
———. *Materialy dlia biografii Pushkina*, 2nd ed. Petersburg, 1873.
Annensky, Innokenty. "The Problem of Gogolian Humor," in *Knigi otrazhenii*. Moscow, 1979.
Ariosto, Ludovico. *The Orlando Furioso*, trans. William Stewart Rose. London, 1828.
Babkin, A., and V. Shendetsov. *Slovar' inoiazychnykh vyrazhenii i slov*, 2nd ed., vol. 2. Leningrad, 1987.
Baratynsky, Evgeny. *Polnoe sobranie stikhotvorenii*. Leningrad, 1957.
Belinsky, Vissarion. *Polnoe sobranie sochinenii v 13 tomakh*, vol. 4. Moscow, 1954.
Bloom, Harold. *The Anxiety of Influence: A Theory of Poetry*. New York, 1973.
Brodsky, Joseph. *Chast' rechi: Izbrannye stikhi 1962–1989*. Moscow, 1990.
———. *On Grief and Reason*. New York, 1995.
Dahl, Vladimir. *Tolkovyi slovar' zhivago velikorusskago iazyka*, vols. 3–4. St. Petersburg, 1882.
Derzhavin, Gavriil. *Stikhotvoreniia*. Leningrad, 1981.
Eichenbaum, Boris. "How 'The Overcoat' Is Made," in *Gogol from the Twentieth Century*, ed. and trans. Robert A. Maguire. Princeton, N.J., 1974.
———. *Stat'i o Lermontove*. Moscow-Leningrad, 1961.
Emerson, Caryl. "Pikovaia dama and Romantic Tragedy by Other Means." Paper delivered at the annual conference of American Association of Teachers of Slavic and Eastern European Languages (AATSEEL), Chicago, December 1985.
Entsiklopediia sueverii. Moscow, 1995.
Gasparov, Boris. *Poeticheskii iazyk Pushkina kak fakt istorii risskogo literaturnogo iazyka*. Vienna, 1992.
Gogol, Nikolai. *Arabesques*, trans. Alexander Tulloch. Ann Arbor, Mich., 1982.
———. *The Complete Tales*, vol. 2, ed. Leonard J. Kent. Chicago, 1985.

———. *Dead Souls: The Reavey Translation*, ed. George Gibian. New York, 1985.

———. *Sobranie sochinenii v deviati tomakh*, vols. 3–4, 6–9. Moscow, 1994.

Gogol from the Twentieth Century, ed. and trans. Robert A. Maguire. Princeton, N.J., 1974.

Gorlin, Mikhail. "Karty v russkoi literature," *Sed'mye Tynianovskie chteniia. Materialy dlia obsuzhdeniia*. Vyp. 9. Riga-Moscow, 1995–96.

Gukovsky, Grigory. *Realizm Gogolia*. Moscow-Leningrad, 1959.

Guminsky, Viktor. "'Taras Bulba' v *Mirgorode* i *Arabeskakh*," in *Gogol: istoriia i sovremennost*, eds. V. Kozhinov et al., Moscow, 1985.

Karatygin, Petr. *Dela davno minuvshikh dnei*. St. Petersburg, 1888.

Karlinsky, Simon. *The Sexual Labyrinth of Nikolai Gogol*. Cambridge, Mass., 1976.

Kireevsky, P. *Sobranie narodnykh pesen*. Leningrad, 1977.

Kotliarevsky, Ivan. *Tvory*. Dnipro, 1980.

Kuleshov, Vasily. *Istoriia russkoi kritiki*. Moscow, 1978.

Kulish, P. *Opyt biografii N. V. Gogolia*. St. Petersburg, 1854.

Lednicki, Waclaw. *Pushkin's "Bronze Horseman": The Story of a Masterpiece*. Berkeley, Calif., 1955.

Legendy i mify o Pushkine. Petersburg, 1994.

Leighton, L. G. "Gematria in *The Queen of Spades:* A Decembrist Puzzle," *SEEJ*, vol. 21, no. 4, 1977.

Lermontov, Mikhail. *A Hero of Our Time*, trans. Vladimir Nabokov. Woodstock, N.Y., 1988.

———. *Sochineniia v 6 tomakh*, vols. 2, 6. Moscow-Leningrad, 1957.

Lotman, Iurii. *Besedy o russkoi kul'ture*. St. Petersburg, 1994.

———. *Izbrannye stat'i*, vol. 2. Tallinn, Estonia, 1992.

———. *Roman A. S. Pushkina "Evgenii Onegin": Kommentarii*. Leningrad, 1980.

Maguire, Robert. *Exploring Gogol*. Stanford, Calif., 1994.

Mann, Iurii. *Smelost' izobreteniia: Cherty khudozhestvennogo mira Gogolia*. Moscow, 1979.

Manuilov, Viktor. *Roman M. Iu. Lermontova "Geroi nashego vremeni": Kommentarii*. Moscow-Leningrad, 1966.

Morson, Gary Saul. "Gogol's Parables of Explanation: Nonsense and Prosaics," in *Essays on Gogol: Logos and the Russian Word*, eds. Susanne Fusso and Priscilla Meyer. Evanston, Ill., 1992.

Nabokov, Vladimir. *Lectures on Literature*. New York, 1980.

———. *Nikolai Gogol*. Norfolk, Conn., 1944.

Orwell, George. *Collection of Essays*. New York, 1954.

Pasternak, Boris. *Stikhotvoreniia i poemy.* Moscow-Leningrad, 1965.

Peace, Richard. *The Enigma of Gogol: An Examination of the Writings of N. V. Gogol and Their Place in the Russian Literary Tradition.* Cambridge, England, 1981.

Plato. *The Collected Dialogues,* eds. Edith Hamilton and Huntington Cairns. Princeton, N.J., 1989.

Plutarch. *The Lives of the Noble Grecians and Romans,* trans. J. Dryden. Chicago, 1952.

Pushkin, Alexander. *Complete Prose Fiction,* trans. Paul Debreczeny. Stanford, Calif., 1983.

———. *Eugene Onegin,* trans. Charles Johnston. Harmondsworth, N.Y., 1979.

———. *Sobranie sochinenii v desiati tomakh,* vol. 2. Moscow, 1974.

Pushkin Threefold: Narrative, Lyric, Polemic, and Ribald Verse, trans. Walter Arndt. New York, 1972.

Pushkin v vospominaniiakh sovremennikov, vol. 2. Moscow, 1974.

Robbins, Rossell Hope. *Encyclopedia of Witchcraft and Demonology.* Edited, revised, expanded, and translated into Russian under the supervision of F. Kapitsa. Moscow, 1995.

Ronen, Omry. "Leksicheskii povtor, podtekst i smysl v poetike Osipa Mandelstama," in *Slavic Poetics: Essays in Honor of Kiril Taranovsky.* The Hague, Paris, 1973.

Rosen, N. "The Magic Cards in *The Queen of Spades*." *SEEJ,* vol. 19, no. 3, 1975.

Rostand, Edmond. *Cyrano de Bergerac: A New Version in English Verse,* trans. Brian Hooker. New York, 1951.

Russkaia elegiia XVIII-nachala XX veka. Leningrad, 1991.

Samsonov, Nikolai. *Drevnerusskii iazyk.* Moscow, 1973.

Shapiro, Georgy. *Nikolai Gogol and the Baroque Cultural Heritage.* University Park, Pa., 1993.

Smirnov, Igor. *Porozhdenie interteksta (Elementy intertekstual'nogo analiza s primerami iz tvorchestva B. L. Pasternaka).* St. Petersburg, 1995.

Sosnora, Viktor. *Nikolai.* St. Petersburg, 1992.

Stilman, Leon. "The "All-Seeing Eye' in Gogol," in *Gogol from the Twentieth Century,* ed. and trans. Robert A. Maguire. Princeton, N.J., 1974.

Suetonius, Gaius Tranquillus. *The Twelve Caesars,* trans. Robert Graves. Harmondsworth, N.Y., 1979.

Tarasenkov, A. T. *Poslednie dni zhizni N. V. Goglia.* Moscow, 1902.

Tarkovsky, Andrei. *Sculpting in Time,* trans. Kitty Hunter-Blair. Austin, Texas, 1986.

Tolstoy, Leo. *War and Peace,* trans. Ann Dunnigan. New York, 1968.

Tsiavlovsky, Mikhail. *Letopis' zhizni i tvorchestva Pushkina: 1799–1826*. Leningrad, 1991.

Turbin, Vladimir. *Pushkin.Gogol.Lermontov: Ob izuchenii literaturnykh zhanrov*. Moscow, 1978.

Venevitinov, Dmitry. *Stikhotvoreniia*. Moscow, 1976.

Veresaev, Vikenty. *Gogol v zhizni*. Moscow, 1990.

———. *Pushkin v zhizni*, vols. 1–2. Moscow, 1936.

Vinitsky, Ilya. *Utekhi melankholii*, vyp. 2. Moscow, 1997.

Vinogradov, Viktor. "Naturalisticheskii grotesk (Siuzhet i kompozitsiia povesti Gogolia 'Nos')," in *Izbrannye trudy: Poetika russkoi literatury*. Moscow, 1976.

Viskovaty, P. M. *Iu. Lermontov. Zhizn' i tvorchestvo*. Moscow, 1891.

Weiskopf, M. "The Bird Troika and the Chariot of the Soul: Plato and Gogol," in *Essays on Gogol: Logos and the Russian Word*, eds. Susanne Fusso and Priscilla Meyer. Evanston, Ill., 1992.

Yermakov, Ivan. "The Nose," in *Gogol from the Twentieth Century*, ed. and trans. Robert A. Maguire. Princeton, N.J., 1974.

Zhukovsky, Vasilii. *Izbrannoe*. Leningrad, 1973.

Index

Aeschylus, 105
Aesopian language: use of by Russian writers, xi
"Aesopian literature," xi
Aksakov, Sergei, 58, 98
Aksakov, S.T. *See* Aksakov, Sergei
Alexander I, Emperor, 23
Alexander of Macedonia, 71
allegory: in works of Gogol, 58–59, 134n11
Alov, V. *See* Gogol, Nikolai
Annenkov, Pavel, 84
Annensky, Innokenty: "The Problem of Gogolian Humor," 57
Antony, Mark, 104
approach to literature: biographical, xi–xii, 5, 8, 9, 118–21, 130; Formalist, vii; Freudian, viii, xi, xii, 57; intertextual, 5, 8, 9, 118, 120–22, 130; of Prague theorists, ix; reader response, vii, ix; structuralist, viii; subjectivist, viii
Ariosto, Ludovico, 71, 78, 81; *Orlando Furioso*, 71–74, 76, (and "The Nose") 74, 76, 82, (and works of Pushkin) 79–80, (Pushkin's translation of) 71, 80–81, 82, 108
Aristotle, 75–76, 91
Auden, W.H.: "Precious Five," 56

Babel, Isaac: *Red Cavalry*, ix
Bakhtin, Mikhail, ix–x
Baratynsky, Evgeny, 15–16, 61; and Italy, 86–89, 92; "To My Italian Tutor" ("Diad'ke-Italiantsu"), 88; "The Omens" ("Primety"), 16; "Prejudice! it is a fragment . . ." ("Predrassudok! oblomok . . ."), 14; "Rome," 86; "The Steamer" ("Piroskaf"), 88
Baroque, the, 136–37n18
Barr, George, 116
Bartenev, Petr, 22
Batiushkov, Konstantin, 61, 63, 71, 81, 82; "Monument," 81
Beaumont, Francis: *Salmacis and Hermaphroditus*, 136n13
Belinsky, Vissarion, 42
Bely, Andrei: *The Craft of Gogol*, 95
Benkendorf, Alexander, 123
Bergman, Ingmar, 3
Bible, the, 6, 8, 19; the book of Ezekiel, 7; the New Testament, 77; the Old Testament, 6; the Song of Solomon, 70
biographism. *See* approach to literature: biographical
Bloom, Harold, 120; *The Anxiety of Influence*, 13
Boggs, J.S.G., vii
Borges, J. L., 102
Briullov, Carl, 30
Brodsky, Joseph, 118; exorcism by, 122–23 (*see also* exorcism: by Brodsky); "Fin-de-siècle," 121–22
Brut, Khoma (in "Viy"). *See* Brutus, Thomas (in "Viy")
Brutus, Markus Junius (Junior): and "Viy," 104–5, 107, 108, 111, 112, 114, 115
Brutus, Markus Junius (Senior), 112
Brutus, Thomas (in "Viy"), 96, 102–3, 109–10, 138n41; death of, 114–15, 117; and parallels with Roman history, 104–8, 109, 111, 112, 114; significance of name of, 116

Index

Bunyan, John: *Pilgrim's Progress*, 28
Byron, Lord, 40, 98

Caesar, Julius, 48, 49; and "Viy," 104–5, 107, 108–9, 111, 112, 115
cards (as fortune-telling), 22–24. *See also* fortune-tellers
cards (as game): double nature of, 22; as gamble with destiny, 21, 34–35, 41; in Lermontov, 40, 41, 43, 46, 49, 50; in Pushkin, 21, 50; in Russian literature, 20–21. *See also* cards (individual); faro
cards (individual): ace, (in Lermontov) 43, 44, 47, 48, 50, (as person) 32, 34, 37, (in Pushkin) 26, 27, 28, 31–32, 34, 35, 37, 38, 39; jack, 35; nine, 35; queen of spades, 27, 28, 31–32, 34, 35, 37, 38, (as person) 32–33; seven, (in Lermontov) 43, 44, 47, 48, 50, (in Pushkin) xii, 26, 27, 28, 34, 35, 39; three, (in Lermontov) 44, 47, 48, 50, (in Pushkin) xii, 26, 27, 28, 34, 35, 39. *See also* cards (as game); faro
Catholicism, 94
Caucasus, the, 51
Cervantes, 71
Chaadaev, Petr, 94
Charlemagne, 55
Charlotta, Tsarina, 51
Chechens, the, 43
Chichikov (in *Dead Souls*), 8, 31, 62–67, 69; attempts to guess identity of, 99–101; and madness, 66–67, 75; meaning of name of, 65, 115, 116, 138n59; as parody of elegiac hero, 62
Cicero, 49
Cirlot, Juan Eduardo, 135n24
Collodi, Carlo: *The Adventures of Pinocchio*, 54
Cummings, E. E., 6

Dahl, Vladimir, 37, 138n60
Dante, 125, 129
d'Antès, 25, 34, 38–39
Death: as character in Pushkin, 36–37, 39
Decembrists, the, 49; uprising of, 17, 81
Derzhavin, Gavrill, 20, 81; "On Luck" ("Na schastie"), 20
Desbordes-Valmore, Marceline, 63
destiny, 109; gambling with, of Lermontov, 42, 45, 49–51; gambling with, of Pushkin, 31, 35, 37, 42; and Gogol, 84, 89; Romantic conception of in *Anna Karenina*, xiii; and Andrei Tarkovsky, 13. *See also* cards (as game): as gamble with destiny; fatalism; omens; predestination; superstitions
Dickens, Charles, viii, 118–19, 120; *David Copperfield*, 119
divination, 24; popularity of in Pushkin's era, 14–15. *See also* cards (as fortune-telling); fortune-tellers
Dolgorukov, Princess, 19
Dorokhov, Rufin, 51
Dostoevsky, Fedor, xii; *The Gambler*, xii; *Writer's Diary*, xi
Doubting Thomas, 116
Drashusova (Karlhoff), Elizaveta Alexeevna: *Diary of the Unknown*, 69
Drevets, 82

Eichenbaum, Boris, ix, 27, 44–45; "How 'The Overcoat' is Made," 103
elegy, the, 60–64
Etkind, Efim, 135n28
Eugene (in "The Bronze Horseman"), 78–79, 80, 82
exorcism, 3–13; by Brodsky, of fear of death, 122–23; definitions of, 3, 119, 121; in film, 9–13; by Gogol, (with complications) 84–85, (of fear of incest) 114, (of fear of insanity) 31, 81–82, 84, (of name) 5–9, (of pride) 7–8, (using the New Testament) 77; by Lermontov, of Pushkin's presence in work, 40; modifications of, 121–30, (concealed prayer) 122–23, 130, (semiconscious) 123, 129–30; by Pushkin, (of fear of insanity) 30–31, 123, (of guilty conscience) 129, (of Kirchof's prophecy) 35, 38, 39, 50–51, (of last period of life) 78, (of superstitions) 16; significance of for writers, xi, 9; by Andrei Tarkovsky, 12–13
Exorcist, The (movie), 3
"extra" in the text, the, vii, x, 3–13; and personal code, 121; psychological dominant as, 4

Falconet, Etienne Maurice, 125
faro, 20–21, 34, 43, 46. *See also* cards (as game)
fatalism, vii, xii; in *Anna Karenina*, xii–xiii;

Index

of Gogol, 84, 92, 113, 116; of Gogol's father, 113; of Lermontov, 51, 52 (in works) 41, 42, 44, 49, 50; of Pushkin, xi, 19, 33, 52; in Russian cultural history, xii. *See also* destiny; omens; predestination; superstitions

Faust (in "Sketches for a Project about Faust"), 36–37, 39

Feast of the Annunciation, the, 134n7

Fish, Stanley, ix

folk beliefs, 19, 24, 29, 49. *See also* cards (as fortune-telling); omens; superstitions

fortune-tellers, xi, 23–25. *See also* Kirchof, Madame (Aleksandra Fillipovna)

Frankenstein (novel), 54

Frank, Joseph, xii

Freudianism. *See* approach to literature: Freudian

Freud, Sigmund, xii; the Oedipus complex, 114

Friedkin, William, 3

Gallienus, Emperor, 91

Glebov, Dmitry, 61

Glechyk, P. *See* Gogol, Nikolai

Goethe, 87, 88; "Mignon," 86, 88

Gogol, Nikolai, xii, 5, 26, 82, 136n12; allegory in works of, 58–59, 134n11; Baroque in works of, 137n18; beauty as defined by, 98; belief in Devil of, 98–99; concept of Rome of, 94, 97, 107, 136n14; death of, 113; departure from Russia of, 58; and destiny, 84, 89; dream device in works of, 67–68; epic as defined by, 71; exorcism by, 5–9, 31, 77, 81–82, 84–85, 114 (*see also* exorcism: by Gogol); face-moon-baking as metaphorical triad in works of, 70–71; fatalism of, 84, 92, 113, 116; fear of own name of, 7–8; Greek and Latin knowledge of, 75; Italy as displaced motherland of, 89, 90–91; Italy as residence of, 53, 61, 89, 92, 99, 116; Italy in works of, 84–86, 88–93, 96, 97–98, (equated with Ukraine) 84, 89–90, 92, 107; and Kafka, 68; and madness, 31, 77, 81–82, (connection of noses to) 75, 82; personal code of, 8–9, 62, 67, 82, 84, 103, 112, 117; Platonism of, 107, 113; as "poet in prose," 4, 62; pseudonyms of, 5–6, 8, 9, 54; psychological dominant of, 6–7, 8, 9, 118, (nose as) 53–54; Pushkin's influence on, 76–77, 78, 81–82; relations with mother of, 6, 112–14; Romanticism in poetry of, 85; sexuality of, 53, 57, 98, 114; significance of names in works of, 65, 93–94, 102–117, 138n59; superstitions of, 84; theme of vision in works of, 109–11. *See also* nose (body part): in Gogol; Ukraine: and Gogol

Gogol, Nikolai, works of: "Al-Mamun," 75; "On Anxiety, Hypochondria and Lack of Confidence" ("O boiazni, mnitel'nosti i neuverennosti v sebe"), 77; *Arabesques*, 69, 75, 96; "Author's Confession" ("Avtorskaiia ispoved'"), 76, 78; "Boris Godunov," 7; "Chapters from the Novel *Hetman*," 6; *Dead Souls*, x, 4, 8, 31, 59, 69, 70, 138n59, (allusions to *Eugene Onegin* in) 63–64, (as contribution to elegiac genre) 62–67, (evil in characters from) 99–101, (madness in) 75, ("nasal" terms in) 64, 66, (and "The Nose") 65–67, (planned second part of) 71, (Pushkin's idea for) 77, (as rewrite of Homer and Dante) 82, ("The Story of Captain Kopeikin") 99–101, 115, 137n34; "The Diary of a Madman," 69–70, 77; *Evenings on a Farm Near Dikanka*, 90; "A Few Thoughts about How to Teach Children Geography," 6; "A Frightful Boar," 5–6; "Ganz Küchelgarten," 5, 53, 85; "A Glance at the Composition of Little Russia," 96–97; "A Horrible Revenge," 90; *The Inspector General*, 7, 58–59, 76, 82, 138n52, (Pushkin's idea for) 77; "Italy," 85, 88–89, 92; *Mirgorod*, 92–96, 97, 99, 114–16, 136n14, (double meaning of title) 93–94, 136n17; "Nevsky Prospect," 31, 54, 59–60, 69, 93, (madness in) 74, ("Schiller-Hoffman" Romantic mode in) 60, 72; "The Nose," 31, 54, 55, 62, 68–71, 72, 115, (critical interpretations of) 56–57, (and *Dead Souls*) 65–67, (first publication of) 76, (madness in) 75–76, 82, (and "Nevsky Prospect") 59–60, (and *Orlando Furioso*) 74, 76, 82; "Old-World Landowners," 94, 95, 114; "The Portrait," 93; "Razviazka Revizora"

147

Index

("The Finale of *The Inspector General*"), 58–59; "Rome," 97–98; *Selected Passages from Correspondence with Friends*, 6; "The Tale of How Ivan Ivanovich Quarreled with Ivan Nikiforovich," 93, 94, 95–96, 114; "Taras Bulba," 7, 71, 90, 92, 94, 96, 114, (as rewrite of Homer) 82, 95; "Teacher," 5; *Textbook of Literature for Russian Youth (Uchebnaia kniga slovesnosti dlia russkogo iunoshestva)*, 71, 72, 78; "On Those of Our Mental Predisposition and Defects That Embarrass Us and Prevent Us from Being Calm" ("O tekh dushevnykh raspolozheniiakh i nedostatkakh nashykh, kotorye proizvodiat v nas smushchenie i meshaiiut nam prebyvat' v spokoinom sostoianii"), 77; "Viy," 94, 96, 98, 99, 102–17, (Roman history and) 103–9, 111, 112, 114, 115–16, 117; "Woman," 6

Gogol, Vasilii Afanasievich, 113, 138n59

Gogol-Ianovskaiia, Mariia Ivanovna, 112–14, 138n59. *See also* Gogol: relations with mother of

Golitsyna, Princess Natalia Petrovna, 26

Goncharova, Natalia, 76. *See also* Pushkin: relations with wife of

Gopnik, A., 102

Gorlin, Mikhail, 20

Gorobets, Tiberius (in "Viy"), 103, 115

Grabbe, Count, 28

Grushnitski (in *A Hero of Our Time*, "Princess Mary"), 45–49, 50

Gukovsky, Grigory: *The Realism of Gogol*, 93

Guminsky, Viktor, 136n17

Hamlet, 66

Hardy, Thomas, 118

O. Henry, ix

Hermann (in *The Queen of Spades*), 26, 33, 35, 37, 42; compared to Vulich (in *A Hero of Our Time*, "The Fatalist"), 43–44; madness of, 21, 27–28, 30; as parodic and serious, 30–32; Russia resembling, xii

Herzen, Aleksandr: *My Past and Thoughts*, 94

Hoffman (in "Nevsky Prospect"), 59–60, 74

Hoffman, E.T.A., 59, 60

Holland, Norman, viii

Homer, 4, 6, 8, 71, 82; *The Iliad*, 71, 137n22; *The Odyssey*, 6

Horace, 81

Ianov, G. *See* Gogol, Nikolai

Iazykov, Nikolai, 53, 61

intertextuality. *See* approach to literature: intertextual

Iser, Wolfgang, viii

Italy: and Baratynsky, 86–89, 92; and Gogol, (as displaced motherland) 89, 90–91, (as residence) 53, 61, 89, 92, 99, 116, (Roman history and "Viy") 103–9, 111, 112, 114, 115–16, 117, (in works) 84–86, 88–93, 96, 97–98; Romantic-era cult of in Russia, 85–87; as setting for *Nostalgia* (film), 9, 11, 12. *See also* Gogol: concept of Rome of; Ukraine: and Gogol (equation with Italy)

Ivanitsky, N., 38, 39

Jakobson, Roman, viii

Kafka, Franz: "The Metamorphosis," 68

Karatygin, Petr, 23

Karlinsky, Simon, 53; on beauty in Gogol, 98; on "The Nose," 56, 57, 59, 134n7, 134n11; on "Viy," 112

Katenin, Pavel, 71

Kern, Anna, 22, 27

Khaliava (in "Viy"), 103, 116–17

Khastatov, Yakim, 133n70

Khokhriakov, Vladimir Kharlampievich, 133n70

Khomiakov, Alexei, 39

Kirchof, Madame (Aleksandra Fillipovna), 23–24, 25, 33–34, 35, 39

Konstantin Mikhailovich, Grand Prince, 24

Kotliarevsky, Ivan: *The Aeneid*, 89–90

Kovalev, Major Platon (in "The Nose"), 56–57, 60, 69, 134n7; awakenings of, 67–68; compared to Pirogov (in "Nevsky Prospect"), 59; compared to Plato, 75; face of resembling pancake, 56, 69, 70; madness of, 76, 82; retrieval of nose by, 74, 82

Kozlov, Ivan, 71

Index

Küchelbecker, Wilhelm, 53–54
Kulish, Panteleimon, 6, 8
Kutik, Ilya, vii, xiii; concepts of, x–xii

Lent, 70
Lermontov, Mikhail, xii, 4, 5, 16, 61, 88; duel in works of, 45–49; exorcism by, 40 (*see also* exorcism: by Lermontov); fatal duel of, 51–52; fatalism of, 51, 52, (in works) 41, 42, 44, 45, 49, 50; gambles with destiny of, 42, 45, 49–51, (in works) 45; personal code of, 40, 48; psychological dominant of, 118; and Pushkin, 39–46, 48, 49–51, 52; similarity to Pechorin, 42, 50; superstitions of, 39–52. *See also* cards (as game): in Lermontov; cards (individual)
Lermontov, Mikhail, works of: "The Death of a Poet," 40; *A Hero of Our Time*, x, 44, ("Bela") 44, ("The Fatalist") 40–46, 47, 48, ("Maksim Maksimich") 44, ("Princess Mary") 44–49, ("Taman") 44; "No, I am not Byron, I am different . . . ," 40; "Valerik," 49–50
Levin, Iurii, 135n28
literature, theory of. *See* approach to literature
Lomonosov, Mikhail, 81
Lopukhin, Alexei, 49
Lopukhina, Mariia, 51
Lotman, Iurii, 21, 22, 26, 35, 63, 103

Maguire, Robert A., 136n14
Mamaev, K. Kh., 51
Mandelstam, Osip, 95, 120
Mann, Iurii, 99
Mansurov, Pavel, 24
Manuilov, Viktor, 45, 49, 50
Martynov, Nikolai, 51–52
Mephistopheles (in "Sketches for a Project about Faust"), 36
Merezhkovsky, Dmitry, 101; "Gogol and the Devil," 98
Mickiewicz, Adam, 32; *Dziady (Forefathers)*, 125–26, 129; *Fragment*, 125; "To My Russian Friends," 127–28, 129; and Pushkin, 125–30
Mirgorod (city), 93–94
Mochul'skii, Pavel, 59
moon, the, 68, 74; cult of, 135n24; nose living on, 70, 71, 75, 82; as omen, 29; in *Orlando Furioso*, 72–73; in Plato, 136n12
Morson, Gary Saul, 56–57
Moskovskii Nabliudatel' (The Moscow Spectator) (magazine), 76
Muravev, Andrei, 25

Nabokov, Vladimir, 49, 53, 68, 98; on Chichikov (in *Dead Souls*), 62, 101
Napoleon, 23, 99, 100, 101, 123
Nashchokin, Pavel, 19
Nature (magazine), 82
Nicholas I, Emperor, 25, 51–52, 58
nose (body part), 83; in Gogol, 31, 53–57, 59–60, (connection to insanity) 75, 82, (in *Dead Souls*) 64–67, 75, (dual role on face of) 69–71, (Kovalev's retrieval of) 74, 82, (as male sexual organ) 57, 134n7, (as symbol of loss) 62, 64–67, (as synecdoche for face) 70–71; living on the moon, 70, 71, 75, 82; in world literature, 54–55, 134n3
nose (philosophical category). *See nus*
Nostrilov (in *Dead Souls*). *See* Nozdrev
Novosiltseva, E., 18
Nozdrev (in *Dead Souls*), 65–66, 69
nus, 75–76, 82, 91, 136n12

Octavian, 104
omens: in *Anna Karenina*, xiii; in *A Hero of Our Time*, 46–49; Pushkin's belief in , 50, (blond hair/white man) xii, 23, 25, 33, 34, 39, (good) 19, (hare) 17–18, (moon) 29, (priest at start of journey) 17, (white horse) 23, 25, 34; stumbling, 49, 137n34. *See also* fatalism; folk beliefs; predestination; superstitions
Orlov, Alexei Fedorovich, 24
Orwell, George: "Charles Dickens," 118–19
Otechestvennye zapiski (Notes of the Fatherland) (periodical), 44
Ovid: *Metamorphoses*, 136n13

palindrome, 67, 75, 94, 136–37n18. *See also* play on words
Pasternak, Boris, 39, 40
Peace, Richard, 136n17
Pechorin (in *A Hero of Our Time*), 40–43, 45–49; similarity to Lermontov, 42, 50

personal code, 9, 12, 130; and biographical approach, 119–21; of Gogol, 8–9, 62, 67, 82, 84, 103, 112, 117; and intertextual approach, 121; of Lermontov, 40, 48; psychological dominant as basis of, 4; of Pushkin, 27–39, 129; of Andrei Tarkovsky, 10–12
Peshkovsky, A., 84
Peter the Great, 78, 125–26
Plato, 75–76, 91, 92, 111, 117, 136n13; androgynous principle of, 107, 136n12; *Meno*, 104, 107; *Symposium*, 71, 92, 136n12. *See also* Gogol: Platonism of
Platonists, the, 76, 91
play on words: *nausea/nossea*, 53, 82, 84; *nos/nus*, 75–76, 82, 136n12; *Rim/mir*, 94; *son/nos*, 67, 75; *urbi/orbi*, 94, 137n19. *See also* palindrome
Pletnev, Petr, 30, 76
Plotinus, 76, 91
Plutarch, 108–9, 115; *Alexander*, 38; *Parallel Lives*, 49, 104
poema, 77, 125, 129; *Dead Souls* as, 4, 62
Pogodin, Mikhail, 17, 25
Polevoi, Ksenofont, 22
Poprishchin (in "The Diary of a Madman"), 69, 71, 75
Prague theorists, the. *See* approach to literature: of Prague theorists
predestination: Pushkin's attempts to avoid, 50; in works of Lermontov, 40–41, 44, 49. *See also* destiny; fatalism; omens; superstitions
Prokopovich, Feofan, 137n18
psychological dominant: as basis of personal code, 4, 9, 121; and biographical approach, 5, 9, 120, 121; of Gogol, 6–7, 8, 9, 118, (nose as) 53–54; and intertextual approach, 5, 9, 120, 121; of Lermontov, 118; of Pushkin, 118, 129; of Andrei Tarkovsky, 10–11
pun. *See* play on words
Pushkin, Alexander, xii, 4, 5, 7, 26, 61, 68, 88; avoidance of predestination of, 50; duality in character of, 30; exorcism by, 16, 30–31, 35, 38, 39, 50–51, 78, 123, 129 (*see also* exorcism: by Pushkin); fatal duel of, 29, 39, 40, 52; fatalism of, xi, 19, 33, 52; and fortune-telling, 23–25, 33, 34, 37–38; and friendship, 128; gambles with destiny of, 31, 35, 37, 42; and Gogol, 76–77, 78, 82; and Lermontov, 39–46, 48, 49–51; and madness, 28–30, (Italian influence on theme in works of) 78–81; magazine founded by, 76; melancholia suffered by, 28–30, 78; and Mickiewicz, 125–30; numerology in works of, xii, 26–27, 31, 51, 132n37; passion for gambling of, 20–22, 30, 34; personal code of, 27–39, 129; Polish uprising in works of, 123–24, 129; psychological dominant of, 118, 129; relations with wife of, 18, 29, 30, 34, 38–39, 78; sister of, 30; superstitions of, xi, 14–19, 22–25, 27, 29, 34, 39 (*see also* omens: believed in by Pushkin)
Pushkin, Alexander, works of: "The Anniversary of Borodino," 123–24; *The Bronze Horseman*, 28, 30, 33, 82, 125, 126, (parallels with *Orlando Furioso*) 80, (theme of madness in) 78–80; *Eugene Onegin*, 15, 17–18, 19, 39, (allusions to in *Dead Souls*) 63–64; "He lived among us . . ." ("On mezhdu nami zhil . . .), 127–28; "Monument," 81; "A Pilgrim" ("Strannik"), 28, 30, 33; "Please, God, do not let me go mad . . ." ("Ne dai mne Bog soiti s uma . . ."), 28, 30, 78, 123; "Poet," 64; *The Queen of Spades*, x, xi, xii, 19, 20–21, 26–39, 51, (compared with *A Hero of Our Time*) 40–44, 48, 50; "Sketches for a Project about Faust" ("Nabroski k zamyslu o Fauste"), 35–36; "To the Slanderers of Russia," 123, 129; "And we went further—and fear embraced me . . ." ("I dale my poshli—I strakh obnial menia . . ."), 125, 129; translations by, (of *Orlando Furioso*) 71, 80–81, 82, 108, (of poems by Mickiewicz) 126–27, (of *The Songs of the Western Slavs*) 127

Raevsky, Sviatoslav, 133n70
Raich, Semen, 72
Rembrandt, von Rijn, 23

Index

Robbins, Rossell Hope, 116
Romanticism, 4, 15, 42, 59, 60, 64, 70; in poetry of Gogol, 85; in Russia, 16, 61, 72, 85–87, 91
Ronen, Omry, 120
Rostand, Edmond: *Cyrano de Bergerac*, 54–55
Russia: fatalism in, xii; Gogol's departure from, 58; madmen as messengers of secret wisdom in, 10; names in eighteenth-century literature of, 103; nostalgia for, 10; popularity of *Orlando Furioso* in, 71; proverbs of, 40, 99; resemblance to Hermann (in *The Queen of Spades*), xii; Romantic cult of Italy in, 85–87; superstitions in, 17, 19, 49, 137n34 (*see also* folk beliefs and omens); suppression of Polish uprising by, 123–24; thinkers of the 1910s and 1920s from, vii; treatment of writers in, ix. *See also* Romanticism: in Russia
Russian Formalists, the. *See* approach to literature: Formalist

Saint Thomas Aquinas, 116
Saltykov, Shchedrin, Mikhail, xi
Samsonov, Nikolai, 136
Schiller (in "Nevsky Prospect"), 59–60, 74
Schiller, Friedrich: *The History of the Thirty-year War*, 59; *Wilhelm Tell*, 59, 60
Servilia (mother of Marcus Junius Brutus Junior), 104, 112
Shan-Girei, Akim Pavlovich, 133n70
Shapiro, Georgy, 137n18
Shevyrev, Stepan, 58
Shrovetide week (*maslenitsa*), 70
Siberia, 81
Silk, M., 137n22
Smirnov, Igor, 13, 120, 121
Sobolevsky, Sergei, 23, 25, 33, 34
Sokolova, V., 135n25
Son of the Fatherland (Syn Otechestva) (magazine), 85, 88–89, 135n1
Sophocles, 105
Sosnora, Viktor, 4, 51
Sovremennik (Contemporary) (magazine), 76

Stilman, Leon, 110, 111, 112
Stolypin, Mongo, 133n70
St. Petersburg University, 91
structuralists, the. *See* approach to literature: structuralist
Sturm und Drang, 60
subjectivism. *See* approach to literature: subjectivist
Suetonius, 105
Sultanov, N.A., 51
superstitions: of Gogol, 84; of Lermontov, 39–52; popularity of in Pushkin's era, 14–15; of Pushkin, xi, 14–19, 22–25, 27, 29, 34, 39; in Russia, 17, 19, 49, 137n34. *See also* fatalism; folk beliefs; exorcism: by Pushkin, of superstitions; omens; predestination
Surrealism, 53, 134n11

Tarasenkov, A. T., 77
Tarkovsky, Andrei, 9–13; *Andrei Rublev*, 10; exorcism by, 12–13; *The Mirror*, 12; *Nostalgia*, 9–13; personal code of, 10–12; psychological dominant of, 10–11; *Stalker*, 10. *See also* destiny: and Andrei Tarkovsky
Tarkovsky, Arseny, 12
Tasso, 81, 87
Tatyana (in *Eugene Onegin*), 15, 17–18, 19, 63
Tchaikovsky, Peter, 26; *Eugene Onegin* (opera), 26
Time (magazine), 82
Tiutchev, Fedor, 88
Tolstoy, Leo: *Anna Karenina*, xii–xiii; *War and Peace*, viii, 51, 100
Tristram Shandy (novel), 54
Trojan war, the, 60
Trollope, Anthony, viii
Turbin, Vladimir, 136n17
Turgenev, Alexander, 130
Tynyanov, Yuri, viii

Ukraine, 136n18; and Gogol, (equation with Italy) 84, 89–90, 92, 107, (in works) 93, 96–98, 117

Valerik, the river, 49, 51
Velichkovskii, Ivan, 137n18

Index

Venevitinov, Dmitry, 88, 91, 92; "A Conversation between Plato and Anaxagoras," 91; "Italy," 86
Veresaev, Vikenty, 53
Viazemsky, Prince, 17, 22, 32, 34, 56, 61
Vinitsky, Ilya, 59
Virgil, 89
Virgin Mary, the, 113
Viskovaty, P., 51, 133n70
Viy (in "Viy"), 111–12
Vsevolozhsky, Nikita, 24
Vul'f, Alexei, 22

Vulich, Lieutenant (in *A Hero of Our Time*, "The Fatalist"), 40–44, 45, 46, 48, 50

Weltanschauung: difference between Pushkin's and Lermontov's, 50; of post-Decembrist era, 44
Weschler, Lawrence, 131n1

Yermakov, Ivan, 57

Zhukovsky, Vasilii, 14, 56, 60, 62, 89, 91; "Svetlana," 14–15

About the Author

The Russian poet Ilya Kutik is a founder and spokesman for the literary nonconformist movement of metarealism in the Soviet Union of the 1980s. His works in English include *Hieroglyphs of Another World: On Poetry, Swedenborg, and Other Matters*, published by Northwestern University Press. He is an associate professor of Slavic languages and literatures at Northwestern University.